THE SWORD AND THE SCIMITAR

ERNLE BRADFORD

THE SWORD AND THE SCIMITAR

THE SAGA OF THE CRUSADES

G. P. PUTNAM'S SONS

This book was devised and produced by
Park and Roche Establishment, Schaan

Published in 1974 by G P Putnam's Sons

Design by Mike Mathews
Picture research by Juliet Brightmore

SBN 399–11375–4
Library of Congress Catalog No. 74–78639

Printed in Italy by Amilcare Pizzi, SA, Milan

Jacket illustration: *the massacre of Peter the Hermit's followers. Fourteenth century French manuscript*

Endpaper illustration: *Templar Knights fighting Saracens. From a wall-painting in the Church at Cressac, circa 1170-80*

Title page illustration: *Richard the Lion Heart unhorses Saladin. From the* Luttrell Psalter, *circa 1340*

Contents

List of colour plates

In the Name of God, the Merciful, the Compassionate

By the night enshrouding
And the day in splendour
And that which created the male and the female,
surely your striving is to diverse ends.

From The Koran. Translated by A J Arberry

Shrines and Pilgrims

The Crusades, those wars between the East and West which shook the Mediterranean area for centuries, still exert their influence. Despite the intervening centuries of Ottoman rule in most of the Near East, despite world wars which have changed whole socio-economic patterns, something has survived. The influence of France in the Levant has never been totally eradicated and, despite the events of the past century, there remains from Damascus to Cairo a patina that is quite perceptible. It is a film produced by the oxidation of the bronze of the East due to air from the Latin North. The same is equally true in reverse.

From 1096 to 1291 successive waves of western Europeans, principally from France, streamed eastward to Palestine and Syria to found kingdoms in the land which they called *Outremer* (Beyond the Sea). This warfare and its successive struggles have been treated, according to the nature of their observers, in romantic, religious, political, cultural and economic terms. They were all of these. They were also part of that pendulum in human affairs which oscillates perpetually between East and West, between the opposing polarities set up by differences of climate, race, religion and culture.

The Crusades were different from other long drawn-out struggles that had preceded them. In the great conflicts of the past the motives can usually be discerned as being based on such things as population pressures, leading to the necessity of acquiring more land, and sheer almost motiveless aggression stemming from the desire of a ruler, or rulers, for personal aggrandisement; thus involving their people in warfare which the majority would happily have avoided, had the choice been open to them.

Opposite: *Alexander the Great, 355-323* BC: *detail from a mosaic found at Pompeii, of the Battle of Issus.*

The Peloponnesian War between Athens and Sparta, for instance, was a territorial and commercial one – lit also perhaps by Pericles's dream of making Athens sovereign in all things. Religious motives did not come into it. The greatest wars in which Greece was ever involved were those against the Persians. These were prompted by the Greeks' intransigence, Persian – and Greek – desire for land, and above all by the desire of the Persian monarchs to ensure their almost godlike position as 'Lord of the Lords of this world'. Alexander's wars of conquest in the East were economically determined in the first instance by hunger for land in rich and fertile Asia Minor; politically determined by the fact that the only way of holding the Greeks together in union was to proclaim an external enemy – Persia, which had done so much harm to

The Emperor Constantine the Great, 306-37.

Greece in the past, and might do so again. Beyond this, and increasing as the giant campaign swept inexorably forward, was the craving of Alexander to justify what he had been told by the priests of Amon, at the Oasis of Siva in Libya, that he was indeed the special, divine child of the Ruler of the Universe. The great wars which rent the Mediterranean world between Rome and Carthage were based on economics. Who was to control this sea and the wealth of the known world? These were also to some limited extent racial, in that the Romans represented a Latin world and the Carthaginians a North African and, above all, a Semitic one. The horrors of Carthaginian, or Punic, religion had no bearing on the issue. Cato the Elder's constant insistence that Carthage must be destroyed was not based on any religious scruples, but merely on the fact that he was convinced there could be no security for Rome until Carthage and its Empire were annihilated.

The Crusades, although at one time and another they contained all the elements implicit in earlier wars, were different. Their source was different. They arose through the desire on the part of Christians to visit the places in which their Saviour had lived during his earthly life. Few could read, but all had been told by their priests of Jesus's own pilgrimage through the world, and of the places that he had sanctified by his presence. As early as the second century, Bethlehem and Jerusalem had become places of pilgrimage. From references in *The History of the Christian Church* by Eusebius, who was bishop of Caesarea in Palestine in the early fourth century, it is clear that it was a common practice for Christians to visit Jerusalem for prayer. Bethlehem and the Mount of Olives also figure as places similarly endowed with religious merit. The reason why there is no mention in these early days of the Sepulchre, or of Golgotha, is that these sites were completely lost under the new Roman city of Aelia Capitolina. This had been erected on the site of Jerusalem after its destruction by Titus in AD 70 (The present sites can be considered as no more than hypothetical). Constantine the Great, after his conversion to Christianity and after making it the state religion with its centre in Constantinople (or Byzantium as the city had formerly been called), did much to ensure that the pilgrimage became an important feature of Christian life. The only holy site in Jerusalem before the time of Constantine was the *Cenacle*, or supper room, where it was believed that Jesus had presided over the Last Supper. This was in the house where Mary, the mother of John Mark, was said to have lived, and where the eleven had assembled after the Ascension.

It was Constantine who gave such a great impetus to the pilgrimage to Palestine. He was as eager as all converts before or since to ensure that his conversion was manifestly evident. So, in a practical manner, he began erasing the traces of the Roman conquest of Jerusalem, and sifting beneath them for evidences of his faith. On all the holy sites that could be identified, or identified by the determination of the believer to find them, he had memorial churches erected. Above the site that was traditionally believed to have been the burial-place of Jesus a city rubbish-dump had sprung up. When this was removed, the cave was discovered in which Joseph of Arimathea was said to have laid the body of the Saviour. Over and above this cave, and Crucifixion Hill itself, the Church of the Holy Sepulchre was built in the first half of the fourth century. Helena, the mother of Constantine, undertook the pilgrimage to Palestine in her later years. It was owing to her, according to later tradition, that the Holy Cross was found. Guided by an old Jew who had a traditional knowledge of the area, the cross was identified as being that of Jesus (the crosses of the two robbers were also found in its company) by the miraculous cure of a sick woman who was laid upon it. Eusebius is silent on the subject, and the story is told by later writers, such as St Ambrose. Along with the cross was found the superscription placed over Jesus's head: this was sent to Constantinople. Much controversy was to ensue as to the number of nails found at the same time, most accounts saying that there were four. One of them is said to have been beaten into the iron circlet that forms the crown of Lombardy.

Some writers of the Early Church, including Jerome, attempted to point out that there was no special virtue in making pilgrimages to, or living in, Jerusalem. The good life can be lived anywhere, it is character and intention that count for merit. But Jerome's own conduct and his long residence in Bethlehem somewhat belied his words, and the attraction of the pilgrimage to the Holy Places never ceased. So many towns and cities, from Sarepta (where the tower of Elijah was shown to visitors) to Caesarea (the houses of Cornelius and Philip) and Hebron (the hut of Sarah and the swaddling clothes of Isaac), claimed their share to fame, places mentioned in the Old Testament ranking second only to those which Christ himself had visited. Just as in the ancient world, where pilgrimages were common – to the Temple of Diana of Ephesus, for example, or historical sites such as the ruins of Troy – so the tradition was carried on into the Christian era. Everywhere, and increasingly throughout the Middle Ages, the tombs of local martyrs were venerated, and miraculous cures attributed to the power of these dead holy men. St Augustine, however, comments that, despite the proliferation of martyrs' tombs in North Africa, he himself had never known of any miracles being wrought by them. Nevertheless, the need implanted in the human being for some form of belief in life beyond the grave, the need for cures for sickness when medicine was almost non-existent, and above all man's credulity caused pilgrimages to flourish.

It was from these early manifestations of 'the pilgrim spirit' that the Medieval Church drew its inspiration. However, unlike the Early Church, the men of the Middle Ages placed an extraordinary trust in the efficacy of relics of the saints, of holy men, of places of particular reverence. Content at first with bringing back a handful of dust from the Holy Sepulchre, or a pressed flower from Golgotha, the desire for evidence of the reality not only of places but of saints and martyrs soon grew into what can only be called a 'religious industry'. Caves and tombs were ransacked for bodies, or even portions of bodies, which, whether they had indeed belonged to those to whom they were ascribed, mattered less than the faith with which they were received in the churches to which they were destined. Thus an offshoot of the pilgrimage proper was the pilgrimage to a shrine or church where relics brought from the Holy Land, from Syria, Egypt or Asia Minor, conferred their grace and exuded the spirit of healing. Not all could afford the time or money to make the long and hazardous journey to Palestine, although

Relief of an armed knight: twelfth-century sculpture from the Church of St Martial, Limoges.

it was always conceded that this was the pilgrimage that above all conferred grace and remission of sins upon the traveller. Rome was second only to Palestine as a place of pilgrimage.

It was the conception of the forgiveness of sins obtainable by making a pilgrimage which distinguished the Medieval Church from that of the founding fathers. The power of the priesthood was evidenced by the fact that in lawless centuries it was only they who could deny transgressors the sacraments, or absolve them from sin. For a serious sin or a crime that was against the State as well as the Church, adultery for example in the first instance, and murder in the second, the priest would refer the penitent to his bishop. He in his turn would specify to which shrines, churches or tombs the sinner should make his pilgrimage, and the devotions that he was to offer. Dependent on the nature of his sin, and dependent also upon the views of the bishop, the penitent might be required to wear a hair shirt or an iron chain about his waist thus proclaiming to all and sundry that he was a sinner. Quite apart from this, men of a religious inclination would often impose upon themselves penitence and pilgrimage. Their view would be echoed by Milton:

> What better can we do, than, to the place
> Repairing where He judged us, prostrate fall
> Before Him reverent, and there confess
> Humbly our faults, and pardon beg, with tears . . .

Yet a further spur to the institution of the pilgrimage was given by the system of indulgences. Indulgence is defined as 'the remission of the temporal punishment which often remains due to sin after its guilt has been forgiven.' From the thirteenth century onwards the indulgence freed the sinner not only from temporal penalty but also from the guilt of his sins. Traffic in indulgences was ultimately to become a source of 'investment' by which considerable fortunes were acquired by the Church. Indulgences might be plenary (total), or partial, according to the terms issued. It is important to recall that the first certain instance of the use of plenary indulgence occurred under Pope Urban II, instigator of the First Crusade. As he put it, at the famous Council of Clermont: 'Whoever shall go to Jerusalem out of pure devotion and not to gain honour or money but to liberate the church of God, the same may count that journey in lieu of every penance'.

This was a powerful weapon to have within one's hands. The usage of it by the Popes throughout the Middle Ages undoubtedly helped to promote the Crusades and contributed to the morale of the men involved. It was not until later that the pardoner, of whom we hear in Piers Plowman among others – he 'who gives pardon for pence pound-meal all' (wholesale) – was to corrupt what had originally been a not unintelligent method of securing obedience to law and order (religious and secular) into a professional business. The office of 'pardoner' was not abolished until the Council of Trent in 1562.

But all these later developments had little to do with the Crusades, at any rate the earlier ones. It is essential to understand the religious motive that inspired men of all classes to 'take the Cross', face immense hardships crossing Europe and then, risking either the power of the Turk in Asia Minor or the dangers of the sea, to make their way to Palestine and the Levant. The religious ideals of the time, far removed though they may appear to be from our own, were not so dissimilar from those which still send men and women to work in leper colonies, to dedicate their lives to teaching or hospital work in climates often uncongenial, unhealthy, and remote from their own. If idealism as well as an eye for land may have prompted many of the upper classes, it was the depressed social conditions in western Europe that made so many of the people emigrate under the sanction of Pope and Church, in search of a land 'flowing with milk and honey'. That their dreams were rarely fulfilled was beside the question. Little but starvation and oppression under their feudal lords awaited them in their homes. In the lands beyond the sea, however, they could always hope to obtain better living conditions, quite apart from the promise given them of salvation in the world to come.

As early as the sixth century bishop Adamnan of Iona had written a treatise *On the Holy Places*, and his example was followed shortly afterwards by the Venerable Bede. On the continent, itineraries and reports of routes and places where the pilgrim might find grace as well as lodging for the night had anticipated modern travel books. By the fourteenth century, long after the Latin kingdoms had been overwhelmed in the Near East, the spirit of the pilgrimage had still not been completely eclipsed. Jehan de Mandeville in his book of travels (circa 1336), which largely describes the ways of getting to Jerusalem and the Holy Land, wrote one of the earliest 'best-sellers' in this genre. It was so popular that it was translated into all the vernacular languages of Europe.

The religious and emotional background of the western kingdoms was clearly ripe for that expansion into the East which might well be called 'an armed pilgrimage'. An additional factor during the tenth century was the Cluniac revival, so-called because it stemmed from the Monastery of Cluny (founded in 910). Here a succession of distinguished abbots set in train a revival of religious thinking and of reform among the monasteries of France. In the enforcement of clerical celibacy, and the suppression of simony, the influence of Cluny was supreme. Next to the Pope the abbot of Cluny was probably the most important figure in the Latin Church. Four of them are venerated as saints.

All the indications were that the tide was set for a European movement Eastward. The goal must inevitably be Jerusalem, Jerusalem which had been in Moslem hands for over four centuries. It had been captured in 637 by the Caliph Omar, second of the Mohammedan caliphs and a former adviser of the Prophet. It was he who had largely transformed Islam from a religious sect into an imperial power. The Mosque of Omar, which he had built, was erected on the original site of Solomon's temple, and contained the rock which reputedly marked the scene of Mohammed's ascent into heaven. Sacred to Moslems, Jews, and Christians alike, the city which the Romans had destroyed had risen once more like a phoenix. Like the phoenix, the allure of its voice was irresistible.

Opposite: *Pope Urban II preaching the First Crusade at the Council of Clermont in 1095: from* Livres des Passages d'Outremer, *fifteenth-century manuscript.*

et auftres faincts lieux la enuiron.
Et les vpiens yshabitans z demou
rans . z que les auftres par eulx
tyranniquement z inhumaine
ment tues . Ils auoient reserue
en infelicieuse vie afin que sur
eulx en loprobre du faint nom
vpien peussent continuer plus
souffisemment leurs infaciables

maulctes . Et comment Ils
les tenoient en tres oprobrieuse
captiuite z seruaige. ou tresgrant
deshonneur z oprobre de tous
les vpiens . Concluant z mon
strant par diuerses raisons tres
euidentes que se faint peuple
vpien ne debuoit plus souffrir
nenduret que ses faincts lieux vet

Thunder in the East

Under the rule of Mohammedan caliphs the treatment of Christian pilgrims to the shrines in the Holy Land had been comparatively favourable. The Mohammedan, though regarding them as misguided in their acceptance of Jesus as the ultimate prophet, was prepared to concede that the Moslem, Jewish, and Christian faiths had a mutual ancestry: they were all 'People of a Book'. Jesus was an accepted prophet of the Lord – as were Moses and others – even though the ultimate revelation had come to the camel-driver's son. Provided that the Jews and the Christians paid their dues and caused no trouble, there was little reason why the three faiths should not coexist within Jerusalem and the Holy Land. Not all felt like this, but generally speaking it was possible to exercise a reasonable amount of tolerance towards people who, though not co-religionists, were certainly not pagans. They took much the same viewpoint on the behaviour required by God of man as did the followers of the Prophet.

All this was to change with the coming of the Turks. This race of hardy, nomadic horsemen out of the deserts of Turkestan had burst upon the Arabic world early in the eleventh century, crossing the Oxus and spreading over the eastern provinces of Persia. Theirs was a power which was destined to shatter the old Arabic world, weakened as it was now by religious dissension and by the decline of the Abbasid Caliphate of Baghdad. The Romans, when their power was waning, had employed other races to stiffen their armies – Franks and Huns, for instance – while the Byzantines had similarly made use of Bulgars, Scandinavians, and even Franks. The Arabs also attempted to halt the decline of their military power by an infusion of new blood. This process, which was

Opposite: *Godfrey de Bouillon and his knights on their way to the Holy Land: from William of Tyre's History, c.1280.*

to have so profound an effect upon history, had begun as early as the ninth century. As Sir John Glubb writes in *The Empire of the Arabs*: 'On 9 August, 833, in the army camp where Mamoon [The Abbasid Caliph of Baghdad] died, his brother Mutasim was proclaimed khalif . . . Seventy years had elapsed since Mansoor had founded Baghdad and had settled in it the Khurasan troops on whom he relied. But the Khurasanis, after the disastrous civil war between Ameen and Mamoon, had abandoned their traditional devotion to the Abbasids. Mutasim felt himself obliged to seek elsewhere for loyal troops. He seems to have disliked the Arabs and placed almost all his reliance on Turkish mercenaries. Many of these were already in service but Mutasim greatly increased their numbers. He imported as many as he could from beyond the Oxus until he had built up a bodyguard of ten thousand of them. He dressed them in splendid uniforms, some of them being entirely clad in silk, while their belts and weapons were inlaid with gold and silver. The recruitment of Turks was entirely different from the previous employment of Khurasanis, for the Persians and the Arabs were Muslims and possessors of high cultures. The Turks came from tribes of barbarians . . .' Nevertheless, the Turks were soon to embrace Islam with an ardour that had faded from Arab hearts. The fiery monotheism of the

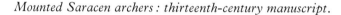

Mounted Saracen archers: thirteenth-century manuscript.

Prophet inspired them. They found an eloquent advocate for their warlike nature in such sayings as, 'Fight in the way of Allah against those who fight against you . . . Kill them wherever you find them . . . Fight the unbelievers totally, even as they fight you.' These 'Seljuk' Turks, called after a famous Turkish chieftain, were soon, like so many other mercenaries, to become the masters of their employers. They captured Khurasan and Baghdad, and in 1055 one of their leaders, Toghrul Beg, had been proclaimed Sultan in Baghdad.

The Turks were not originators, they were not, as the Arabs had been before them, interested in the arts or science, they were warriors. They inherited through their conquests, however, the whole cultural world of Islam, the religion, the architecture, and the literature of the Arabs and the Persians. To these they added little but their dour courage and their capacity for warfare. During the years when the Normans were expanding throughout southern Italy and Sicily, coming into conflict with the Byzantines over those territories which had formerly been part of the great empire administered from Constantinople, the Turks in the East were laying the foundations of their Empire. This would ultimately engulf all these territories in Asia Minor which had nourished the Byzantines for so many centuries. It is easy to see by hindsight that, threatened both in Europe and Asia, the Byzantine Empire, which for so long had been the shield of Christendom in the East, securing the pilgrims' routes, would certainly be unable to contain both threats. Men like Count Roger the Norman by his conquest of Sicily heralded the steady decline of Moslem power in the western Mediterranean. But at the same time such Norman successes indirectly assisted the Turks to complete the conquest and subjugation of the East.

The Empire of the Seljuk Turks and, even more, that of the Ottoman Turks who succeeded them, was to dominate the history of the Mediterranean basin for centuries to come. In 1076 the capture of Damascus and Jerusalem marked the writing on the wall for the Christian pilgrimages. The Turks were not as tolerant or easy-going as many of their Arab predecessors had been. For them the Christians – these 'Franks' from the North – were heretics, unbelievers, and a threat to the monolithic power of Turkish dominated Islam. Alp Arslan, who succeeded Toghrul Beg as Sultan of Baghdad, was one of the greatest warlords of Turkish history. It was he above all who, by annihilating the Byzantine army, paved the way for the Turkish Empire in Asia and, though not for many centuries to come, the ultimate establishment of Turkey in Europe.

The battle of Manzikert, near Lake Van in Armenia, in 1071 was one of the most significant in history. It not only sealed the fate of the Byzantines in the East, but it was to prove the fuse which ultimately set in train that great explosion – the Crusades. Although the Byzantine Empire managed to exist, in a much depleted form, for a further four centuries, it was in essence doomed from the moment when the Emperor, Romanus Diogenes (the combination of Roman and Greek names indicates the nature of the Empire) marched into Armenia. His forces, consisting of Byzantine cavalry and infantry, as well as Germans and Franks, numbered about 60,000. Against him Alp Arslan opposed a force of 100,000, consisting mainly of archers mounted on horseback. The superb horsemanship of the Turks, who rode lightly-clad to war much in the same fashion as their ancestors had stormed out of the steppes, their mobility and the deadly accuracy of their archery, proved too much for the heavier and slower-moving Byzantines. The Emperor himself was brave but impetuous. Instead of maintaining an unbroken front, he forgot the words of a wise predecessor on the throne – 'Beware of surprise and keep the flanks and rear well-guarded'. The Byzantine advance guard fell into an ambush, and all its men were lost. The Turks, well aware that their strength lay in their mobility, refused to close with the more heavily armoured Byzantines. Finally, after a confusion of orders which left his front line open to attack from the rear, Romanus was decisively defeated and himself taken prisoner. It was a disaster from which the Empire never recovered. By 1080 the old Byzantine army, which had kept the frontiers for so many centuries, had practically ceased to exist. If the Holy Places were to be open again to pilgrims, and if Europe itself was to be safeguarded from this formidable power that had swirled up like a dust-storm out of Asia, it was clear that some fresh measures must be taken.

Two years after Manzikert, the new emperor, Michael VII, appealed to Pope Gregory VII for assistance against the Turks. He asked for western troops to recover Asia Minor for Byzantium, in return for which he would ensure a union between the Eastern and Western Churches. This naturally appealed to the Pope but, although he managed to raise a considerable army for this purpose, disputes and local wars in Europe compelled its disbandment. The precedent had been set, however, for the military power of western Europe to be loaned to

Opposite: *Byzantine Gospel: eleventh-century. The binding on this manuscript is typical of Byzantine craftsmanship being made of gold, and inlaid with enamels and precious stones.*

23

the eastern empire in exchange for reciprocal favours. The seed of the Crusades had been sown.

The history of the Crusades can hardly be understood without some reference to the basic causes that underlay the dispute between the Christians of the East and those of the West. Without this it is impossible to comprehend the attitudes of Westerners and Easterners in their suspicion of one another. As the tide of the war in Spain against the Moslems gradually ebbed in favour of the Spaniards, it became a forerunner of the Crusades in that Pope Gregory VII invited all Christian knights to help their brethren in expelling the infidel. By the close of the eleventh century, at the time when the First Crusade against the Moslems in the East was proclaimed by Urban II, the concept of the holy war was familiar in western Europe. Saint Augustine himself had said in *Civitate Dei* that there was such a thing as a justifiable war provided that it was fulfilling the commandments of God. What exactly these were – and are – can be debated to this day.

The Eastern Church tended to regard all war as evil – something to which recourse should only be made as a last resort, when diplomacy and bribery had failed. At once a psychological difference becomes apparent between the Byzantines and the Latins. The Byzantines had, over the centuries, often come to terms of accommodation with their many enemies from East, West, and North. They were shrewd and pragmatic, and well aware that they could not contain all their frontiers solely by weight of arms. They traded with the Moslem, and they were prepared to accept his difference of belief provided that some form of harmony, at least on the surface, could exist between their respective creeds. They held the frontiers, they had done so for centuries, they knew in practice exactly what problems confronted a Christian power in dealing with the enemy. Norman nobility, as well as the Pope, hundreds of miles removed, and totally ignorant of the mental climate of the East, had no conception of what was necessary in order to preserve a *modus vivendi* with the Moslem, whether Turk or Arab.

Constantinople was, as its founder had called it, the New Rome, the successor of the Rome of the pagan Emperors. But in Constantinople there existed an unbroken line of Christian Emperors dating from its foundation in 330. Rival claimants to seniority in the East were Alexandria and Antioch. Jerusalem, while considered by some the younger, had the distinction that it was not only the holiest city of all, but that its first Bishop had been James the Just, brother or half-brother of Christ. Rome, on the other hand, with its innumerable associations with early Christianity – including being the resting place of St Peter and St Paul –

24

claimed supremacy over all the patriarchates of the East. Constantinople, by reason of not having fallen captive to the Arabs, had definitely become the head of all the Christian churches in the East. It contested the right of Rome to speak for all Christendom. There were disputes also on matters of Church ritual and liturgy, the Greek Church from Constantinople refusing to accept the elevation of the Son to an equal position with the Father and the Spirit in the Creed. The dream of the papacy was a universal church which acknowledged Rome as its head. This was something that Constantinople was unprepared to concede.

This division between the Eastern and Western branches of Christianity was accentuated by the difference between the inhabitants of Latin Europe and Greek Byzantium. The Greeks rejoiced in their

The consecration of the third abbey church at Cluny by Pope Urban II in 1095 : the Pope stands on the left of the altar, and Abbot Hugh on the right.

manifest civilization, the heir of all that was best in old Rome and ancient Greece. They were very different peoples; the Greeks quick and volatile, sharp in business and not above making many concessions to the Eastern world with which they were in day-to-day communication. The Latins, on the other hand, and especially those who came from western areas like the Normans of France, were brash, buccaneering, and only a stage or two removed from their violent Nordic ancestors, the Vikings. The Greeks considered them barbarians. The Norman, clasping the sword which had made him master of England, southern Italy, and Sicily, felt only contempt for men who wore silks and jewels. These Byzantines lived in conditions where luxury had surely enfeebled their manliness and, furthermore, they traded regularly with the heretic enemy.

It was clear from an early stage that, if the Battle of Manzikert had reduced the Greeks to such a condition that they had to beg for help from the West, they would not be allowed to forget their indebtedness. The Greeks had called in the New World to redress the balance of the Old. The terms would, as always in such cases, ultimately be set by the deliverers.

Crusader's cross, carried by pilgrims on the First Crusade.

Preaching the Crusade

Alexius Comnenus, who became Emperor of the East in 1081, was thirty-three. He had served with distinction against the Seljuk Turks and in a number of other campaigns in Asia Minor. Early in his reign he had had to face the aggression of the Normans in his western territories, where Robert Guiscard, Duke of Apulia, had captured Corfu and Dyracchium and was laying siege to Larissa in Thessaly. This threat was removed by Robert Guiscard's death, but Alexius at no time had any illusions about the Normans. He knew their wanderlust, their desire for territory and their fighting abilities. He had few illusions about anything.

He had taken over the throne at a time when Byzantine fortunes were at a very low ebb. Furthermore the Byzantine court over which he ruled was a hotbed of intrigue and treachery. At a time when all his energies were needed for concentration on foreign affairs, he always had to keep a watch behind his back to ensure that he was not about to be deposed or murdered. Probably the greatest statesman of his age, he had learned during his youth, when he had to campaign with inadequate forces (and they were not always very reliable), that a man's wits are often more useful than his sword-arm. He had dignity and a gracious manner, and his life reveals a man who was averse to punishing offenders, kindly, but completely cynical wherever the interests of his country were involved. The Normans might have more strength and better weapons, but when it came to politics, statesmanship, or downright duplicity, Alexius could more than hold his own. His daughter, Anna Comnena, in her *Alexiad* not unnaturally painted a flattering portrait of her father, but it is borne out by other authorities, including an anonymous Greek writer, who described him as 'great both in will and in deed.' This was the man who was to set in train the First Crusade.

Pope Urban II, to whom Alexius appealed for help in the East, had inherited somewhat similar circumstances to those which faced the Emperor. The Normans supported him, but Rome was held by an anti-Pope (whom Urban was not able to displace until 1093). Henry IV, the western Emperor, supported the anti-Pope and it was not until the revolt of Henry's son that Urban can have felt any security from his German enemy. Like Alexius, however, he was a calm and intelligent man and, once he had secured his position in Rome, he was able to look around the horizons of Christendom with a realist's eye. Negotiations were opened with the Byzantine court, and at the Council of Clermont held in France in 1095 the Pope declared his hand. Up until then the Council, which was attended by 300 leading clerics, had been concerned with such matters as clerical marriage, the excommunication of King Philip of France for adultery, and the condemnation of simony. But on Tuesday, 27 November, the Pope in person made the announcement that was to determine the future of many thousands of men for years to come. He preached the First Crusade.

Urban took good care that his address was not just made to the assembled clerics. It was to be a public announcement, and the crowds which assembled to hear what the Pope had to say were numbered in their thousands. There were far too many to be accommodated in the cathedral, so the papal throne was taken to an open space outside the city where everyone could hear. But, in view of the crowd, one must assume that the text of the message was passed on later to many of them by listeners who had been, as it were, in the first seats. At least three chroniclers seem to have been present at that time, while a number of other and later versions exist. William of Malmesbury, the best English historian of his day, provides a version which contains what may reasonably be assumed as the basic content of the Pope's message. He told his listeners of the peril which threatened Christendom in the East. The Turks, he said, were advancing into Christian territory, Jerusalem lay captive to them, and pilgrims who attempted to make their way to the Holy Places were suffering indescribable hardships. Brother must help brother – the Western Church must go to the rescue of the Eastern. So much of Asia and the East was already occupied by the enemies of God, and so small a part was occupied by Christians. 'Why fear death,' he said in a famous passage, 'when you rejoice in the peace of sleep, the pattern of death?' This was comprehensible enough, even if hardly good theology. 'It is surely insanity to endanger one's soul through lust for a short space of living. Wherefore rather, my dearest brothers, if it is necessary lay down your lives for your brothers. Rid the sanctuary of God of unbelievers, expel the thieves and lead back the faithful. Let no

Alexius I Commenus, 1081–1118: detail from a mosaic in Santa Sophia, Constantinople. The Emperor's appeal to Pope Urban II for help against the Turks led to the First Crusade in 1095.

loyalty to kinsfolk hold you back; man's loyalty lies in the first place to God. No love of your native soil should delay you, for in one sense the

29

Henry IV, the Western Emperor and the Anti-Pope Clement III : from Otto of Freising's Chronicle, *c.1156.*

whole world is exile for the Christian, and in another the whole world is his country. So exile is our fatherland and our fatherland exile.' . . . .

Urban was a great orator, and he was also an impassioned believer in what he said. The combination produced an irresistible spell. Hardly had he finished, than the cry went up on all sides: 'God wills it! God wills it!' The Bishop of Le Puy fell on his knees before the Pope, imploring him to allow him to go on the expedition. Urban looked upon his enthusiasm with some favour. He had already determined that the leadership must be seen to come from the Church, and must not fall into the hands of the princes and nobles. Its head must certainly be an ecclesiastic. In due course Adhemar, Bishop of Le Puy, would find himself the papal legate. A man of middle age, he had already made the pilgrimage to Jerusalem, and as events were subsequently to show, he was a man of sense whose actions were always designed to control the passions of rivals, and to promote the unity of the Christian cause. A clever and diplomatic prelate, he was nevertheless to find that the farther into the East the army advanced, the less did his position and the authority of the Pope weigh upon the consciences or actions of the military leaders.

Even Urban, perhaps, had hardly counted upon the wave of enthusiasm that now swept France. Men had been waiting for a sign, for some cause to which they could whole-heartedly devote themselves; away from the petty preoccupations of local affairs, and the fighting and feuding between barons and princelings that bedevilled the state of Europe. The Crusade, as Urban no doubt hoped, would, quite apart from its primary objective, channel the warlike energies of the Normans into the cause of liberating Jerusalem and the Holy Places. But many of

30

the nobles, despite their religious inspiration, also retained thoughts of secular advancement. They envisaged new fiefs and lands to add to those which they already owned at home; possessions which they might pass on to their sons for the enrichment of their families and their names. For the mass of Crusaders the religious motive remained supreme. Yet, even among poor townsmen or peasants, there could well be a hope for some material improvement in their lot. Recent years had been bad throughout most of Europe, with famine and pestilence stalking the continent. As Sir Ernest Barker put it: '[It was] no wonder that a stream of emigration set towards the East, such as would in modern times flow towards a newly discovered gold-field – a stream carrying in its turbid waters much refuse, tramps and bankrupts, camp-followers and hucksters, fugitive monks and escaped villains, marked by the same motley grouping, the same fever of life, the same alternations of afflu-ence and beggary . . .' Yet it was not only materialism that lay at the roots of that extraordinary phenomenon known as the Crusades. Certainly it can be said of the First Crusade that it was primarily *un fait ecclésiastique,* and only secondly determined by worldly motives.

Urban himself, having further conferred with his bishops, laid down in Council that plenary indulgence should be granted to all those who took part with the genuine intention of fighting a holy war. As a symbol of this, each man taking part was to wear a red cross on his surcoat, the outer garment which was worn over the armour or mail. Hence the expression 'to take the cross' entered into the languages of Europe. If a man took the cross but failed to set out with the expedition, or turned back rather than die with his face to the enemy, he risked excommunica-tion. As a guarantee to the landowners that no one should steal or other-wise interfere with their properties while they were away, their local bishops were made responsible for their lands and personal possessions. All were to be prepared to set out after harvest-time in the following year, 1096, and were to make Constantinople their assembly-point.

As it turned out, both Pope and Byzantine Emperor were to be aston-ished by the subsequent sequence of events. The Pope had called for an orderly army, led by the great nobles of the time, to go to the assistance of Christendom in the East. Alexius, familar as he was with the use of mercenaries in Byzantine armies, had expected a body of men who owed allegiance to him alone and whom he would pay, or who would draw their pay in the loot of the cities that they captured. Neither could have expected that the results of Urban's address at Clermont would lead to that astonishing forerunner of the First Crusade proper – the People's Crusade.

While the great nobles were raising their forces, even pledging their lands and possessions to obtain the necessary money, and while arrangements were being made with the great maritime republic of Genoa for ships to transport the Crusaders to Palestine, the unlooked for had happened. Inspired by the Pope's conception of a holy war against the Moslem – whether Turk or Arab – itinerant preachers had been taking his words throughout the highways and byways of Europe. Foremost among these was the celebrated Peter the Hermit who, in company with a number of other similar enthusiasts in France and Germany, took Urban's words to the illiterate masses of their countries. The latter, as has been seen, were for various reasons waiting for a sign, something that could promise them a little hope to offset the monotonous harshness of their lives.

Peter, as described by contemporaries, sounds singularly unattractive to look at, but he possessed that inexplicable magic which captures people's innate beliefs and inspires their imaginations. He was an elderly man of French extraction, short, but with a long lean face somewhat resembling that of the donkey which carried him. Clothed only in a long cape, and that not always too clean, Peter, as one who knew him wrote, 'seemed somehow semi-divine both in his actions and his words'. Gathering disciples as he went, Peter was preaching the Crusade throughout France within weeks of Urban's address. He despatched the converts to his belief into other areas of the country, while he himself moved onward with his followers to Cologne and Germany. Within a short time he is said to have made 15,000 converts, all of whom were prepared to make their way to the Holy Land. Meanwhile, other prominent preachers like Walter Sans-Avoir (Have Nothing) were carrying their own version of the papal call throughout Europe. It was not without dismay that, as his daughter wrote, Alexius Comnenus heard that 'All the West, even the barbarians who dwell beyond the Adriatic, out as far afield as the Pillars of Hercules [the Gibraltar Strait] are on the move, bringing their whole families with them'. The Pope, for his part, must have been almost equally disturbed. This aspect of the Crusade – the march of the people – was something that he had neither anticipated, nor could control.

In the spring of 1096 Peter halted for some time at Cologne. Even he had now become aware that, if man does not live by bread alone, he certainly needs an adequate supply of it. The cities and townships of eleventh century Europe were in no way equipped to deal with the sudden arrival of thousands of newcomers, many of them penniless, and many of them perfectly prepared to steal for their necessities. Meanwhile Walter Sans-Avoir and his followers, who had set off before Peter, had asked permission of the King of Hungary to pass through his territories. They had done so without giving any notable offence, and were already on the borders of Byzantine territory. Alexius, even though he had efficiently established stores of provisions at all the main places through which he had expected the Crusade to pass, was hardly prepared for this advance swell, forerunner of the storm that was soon to thunder over the East. He now learned that this ill-assorted rabble of men, women, and even children, was soon to be followed by a further, and even larger, similar contingent. Peter the Hermit, having converted a number of lesser German nobility to his cause as well as the ordinary people, had by now set out from Cologne and was headed eastwards.

Peter the Hermit prays before embarking on the People's Crusade.

There was trouble on the passage through Hungary, a town was stormed, and Peter's adherents were forced to move on quickly to escape the reprisal of the King.

The rest of their passage was marked by similar incidents, not all of them minor. Indeed, the movement of the followers of Walter Sans-Avoir and Peter the Hermit through Europe might well be compared to the passage of a plague of locusts. It was not until early in August 1096 that the two sections of the People's Pilgrimage met outside the walls of Constantinople. Alexius, anxious to assess the character and capabilities of the man who seemed to be the prinicpal leader, received Peter at Court. In the sophisticated and luxurious surroundings of the imperial palace Peter must have cut a strange figure. Lean, ugly, burned brown by the sun, his ragged cloak must have stood out amid the silks and splendours of the Byzantine courtiers like the reminder of another age. He *was* from another age – one that the Byzantines had long put behind them – the age of simple and credulous faith which, it was supposed, could move mountains.

Alexius was very dubious that it would have much effect upon Turks. Nevertheless, some action was required of him. The pilgrims were eating up his country and causing widespread trouble and dismay, and he as Emperor was responsible. He decided that the best thing he could do was to get them clear of the immediate surroundings of Constantinople. He would ship them across to Asia Minor, and let them live off the land there, before they went out against the enemy. He cannot in his heart have had much optimism as to their success.

Opposite: *The taking of Jerusalem by the Crusaders in 1099. Christ is shown in the centre, raising his hand in blessing : from a thirteenth-century manuscript.*

People and Princes

Within a few days of their arrival the combined forces of the pilgrim-crusaders were ferried across the Bosporus by the Byzantine navy and accommodated at Cibotos on the Gulf of Nicomedia. Alexius was no doubt overjoyed to see them gone. The place where they had been set ashore contained an old army encampment, the area was fertile, and regular communications including the supply of provisions could be easily arranged from Constantinople. Perhaps, Alexius may have hoped, they would reform themselves from a disorganised rabble into something approaching a disciplined force. The women, children, and the infirm could be left behind at Cibotos while the others in due course could take the field against the Turks. He cannot have had much optimism as to the outcome, for he knew well enough the efficiency and courage of the Seljuks. At any rate he had relieved Constantinople of their awkward presence. He could now await the arrival of the army that Pope Urban had promised him, trained fighting men under the command of great nobles who, having pledged themselves to him as their overlord, would recapture the lost lands of Byzantium. True, he knew that some of them would endeavour to carve out for themselves petty kingdoms and principalities in Asia Minor and the East, but he had confidence that they could, like previous Norman adventurers before them, be contained within the web of Byzantine diplomacy. In the meantime he urged Peter the Hermit to keep his followers under control and to make no move until the main body of the Crusaders should have reached Constantinople.

Unfortunately, there was little or no discipline among the hopeful thousands who had left their homes sustained by a dream. The night-

Opposite: *The Church of the Holy Sepulchre and the Dome of the Rock, Jerusalem: from the* Book of Hours *of Rene of Anjou, c.1436*.

mare aspect of their situation had begun to dawn on them in Europe, but now that they were in Asia – and still so far from that promised Jerusalem – such organisation as had ever existed began to collapse completely. The polyglot nature of the People's Crusade did not help, and Peter's sway over his followers suffered a rapid decline, particularly as its members swiftly began to divide into their racial groups. Soon they were raiding the countryside around Cibotos. On one occasion a large band of Frenchmen got as far as the important town of Nicaea, where they had some success in pillaging the outskirts and, if report was correct, massacring the Greek Christians who fell into their hands. Shortly after this, in the September of 1096, the Germans made an expedition into the interior where, after being invested by a body of the Turkish army in a castle which they had captured, they were nearly all killed. Only those who renounced the aims with which they had so hopefully set out, and apostasised, were spared and despatched into captivity.

Peter meanwhile had gone to Constantinople where he hoped to improve relations with Alexius, secure some further guarantees about the transport of provisions, and possibly also find out what news there was of the progress of the army under the princes. His own authority had completely collapsed among the pilgrims, whom he had seduced from their lands and homes by his visions of the Holy Land. It had become evident that those shining towers, those sacred places, were nothing more than a mirage conjured up out of the hot immensities of Asia. In his absence the other leaders came to the conclusion that they could no longer stay at Cibotos, living off the countryside and making sporadic forays against the enemy. They must leave the sick and the women and children behind, and sally out to give battle.

Only by a decisive victory over the Turks could they smash their way through to some city like Nicaea, where they could winter and regroup themselves for the long march south through Asia in the spring. Their situation was indeed intolerable, but the die had been cast from the moment that they had made their way into Byzantine territory and, above all, from the moment when they had embarked in the imperial transports and set foot on this alien shore.

At dawn on 21 October some 20,000 men – the forerunners of all those who would follow in the Crusades throughout the centuries – marched out of camp. Undisciplined, many of them poorly armed, they marched to their death, the knights riding at their head. They were confident only in the belief that their cause and the Cross would inevitably lead them to victory.

Crusaders bombard the city of Nicaea with their captives' heads: from Les Histoires d'Outremer, *thirteenth-century.*

The result was a foregone conclusion. The mounted Turks, accustomed to the disciplined Byzantine armies – and they felt confident that they could annihilate even those – fell upon the Christians in a narrow valley. The mounted knights were attacked with showers of arrows, killing many of the horses, and then as this armoured advance guard cracked and crumpled, the Turks swooped down on the main body from both sides of the valley. A complete rout followed, the survivors, whether on horse or on foot, making their way back as fast as they could to the only security they knew, the camp at Cibotos. Hard on their heels came the Turks.

The confusion that ensued as the panic-stricken survivors poured into the camp was indescribable. The sick, the old, women and children, all of whom had been waiting for the news that the Turk was routed and that the way now lay open to the East, stared into the harsh face of massacre. Most of them were killed, a few enslaved – particularly attractive youths and young girls designed for sale to harems or to

Coronation of Charlemagne: Les Grandes Chroniques de France, *c.1460.*

pleasure some soldier. The destruction of the first Christian forces to enter Asia Minor was complete. A few thousand, all that were left, managed to make their way to a deserted castle on the seashore. Here, with hastily repaired and improved defences they managed to hold out until Alexius, who had heard of the disaster from a Greek sailor, ordered out the navy's galleys to take off the survivors. At the sight of these men-of-war advancing implacably across the ruffled sea, the Turks – who knew the efficiency of their weapons (which included liquid fire – a forerunner of the modern flamethrower) – withdrew from the castle and joined their fellows inland. For them it had been a highly successful day, one in which they had routed and killed so many heretic Franks. They had heard that the Emperor across the water had summoned yet more Europeans to do for him what his own men could no longer do – face the mounted Seljuk in battle. Well, if these bodies and these slaves were typical of the others that were reported to be following, they had little cause for worry. The survivors of Peter's army, quartered in one of the suburbs of the great city, had learned a bitter lesson. Faith was not enough. The road to Jerusalem was a hard one, and the Holy City itself would never be captured by dreams. Peter himself, bereft of hope and of supporters, waited in the ante-rooms of the palace for the armoured men whose pragmatism might salvage the Christian cause.

It is not impossible that Alexius was somewhat relieved to have the burden of this undisciplined rabble removed from the shoulders of his kingdom. He had viewed them with misgiving from the very first. They were not at all what he had asked for, and their undisciplined behaviour and their ill-treatment of his own subjects had hardly endeared them to him. He could only hope that the real army, when it arrived, would prove quite different. Although he was still to have his troubles, political, religious and in practical matters of supply and material, the Emperor would have been heartened if he could have seen the force that was already moving through Europe.

The total number of men who finally reached the city is given by various authorities of the time: the Pope estimating them at 300,000, the contemporary chronicler Fulcher at 600,000. The lower figure is probably more accurate, and even this is perhaps nearly double the amount of fighting men who congregated in Constantinople for what was to be the army of the First Crusade, or 'The Crusade of the Princes' as it has been called.

The army came in four main divisions. The first was under the command of Godfrey de Bouillon, Duke of Lower Lorraine. In company with his two brothers Eustace, Count of Bologne, and Baldwin, he rode at the head of an army of 10,000 cavalry and 30,000 foot soldiers. Godfrey was about 36 years old, a tall handsome man, fair haired and bearded, seemingly the embodiment of the Northern knight – a Viking in the armour of the Christian Middle Ages. Events were to show that Godfrey lacked personality and that he was middling or indifferent as a soldier. His younger brother Baldwin, on the other hand, was a cold character with a determination to found a kingdom in the East (unlike the others he had even brought his wife and family with him). He was to pursue his ambitions with a directness that would ensure his success. He had a taste for culture, and had spent some years as a cleric, having originally been intended for the Church, but he had put this aside in order to serve under his elder brother.

Godfrey took what was known as 'the route of Charlemagne', through Hungary to Constantinople, Charlemagne having been an ancestor of his. It is probable that Eustace of Boulogne travelled through Italy. After a meeting with the King of Hungary, the latter not unnaturally concerned about the passage through his lands of any further Crusaders after his experience of the first, Godfrey and his troups were allowed to proceed. He insisted on severe discipline and warned the men that any who were found looting or stealing would be hanged. They passed through Hungary without incident, crossed into Byzantine territory and reached Constantinople on 23 December 1096. This was Alexius's first real sight of the kind of men that he had summoned up out of the West. Like other magicians, he was to find that the genie of the lamp was not always congenial or amenable to his demands.

Raymond of Toulouse, the first prince to join the Crusade, set out later than Godfrey and he and his force did not reach Constantinople until the following April. Married to Elvira of Aragon, he was a man of sixty, with considerable experience behind him of campaigning against the Moslems in Spain. Pope Urban had, as it were, acknowledged his superiority over the other leaders by taking him into his confidence and privately discussing the aims of the Crusade. Raymond, for his part, felt that he should be the overall leader, but Urban was determined that the leadership should remain in papal hands and that his Bishop, Adhemar of Le Puy, should represent him in this capacity. There was nothing that Raymond could do but agree. He made sure, however, that the papal delegate rode in his company. No doubt he hoped that, as the Crusade moved into action and the secular arm became paramount, he would achieve his ambitions without argument.

Bohemund of Taranto, the ruler of the district of Apulia in south-eastern Italy, was the eldest son of Robert Guiscard. He was the man whom Alexius feared more than any other. His uncle was Roger, Count of Sicily, and both he and Bohemund's father had been conspicuous in their warfare against the Byzantines and in their annexation of what had formerly been the Emperor's lands. At the head of a formidable group of Norman knights, and followed by a large number of Italian mercenaries and volunteers, Bohemund had been slow to respond to the challenge of the Crusade. But when he saw from the evidence of the volunteers pouring southward through Italy that the movement was something he might well turn to his own advantage, he too took the Cross. Like Baldwin, he also envisaged cutting out for himself a powerful kingdom in the East, something immeasurably superior to Apulia. Crossing by

Opposite: *Robert Curthose, Duke of Normandy : detail of a wooden effigy in Gloucester Cathedral.*

43

sea from Bari, he marched overland to Constantinople in winter, reaching the capital in April, at about the same time as Raymond of Toulouse. His force, though smaller than that of Godfrey de Bouillon, was very well-disciplined and well-armed. Bohemund would permit no looting on the way, maintained a firm hold over his followers, and was careful to send ambassadors ahead of him to announce his approach to Alexius.

The fourth main division had set out from northern France in October 1096. It was under the command of Robert, Duke of Normandy, the eldest son of William the Conqueror. Robert was an easy-going, spendthrift character, who had had to raise the money for the expedition by mortgaging the Duchy of Normandy to William Rufus of England. He was on far from good terms with the latter, having been engaged in intermittent warfare with him ever since the death of the Conqueror. William Rufus certainly stood to gain if Robert failed to return from the Crusade or even if, by acquiring territory in the East, he became so involved that he could not attend to his affairs back in France. Robert's adhesion to the Crusade was prompted by genuine religious motives and Urban, anxious to have his support, had managed to effect a reconciliation between him and William Rufus before Robert left for the East. Stephen of Blois and his brother-in-law, Robert of Flanders, Odo, Bishop of Bayeux, and a number of other distinguished members of the nobility, were among his followers. All in all, his division comprised a good cross-section of the Norman rulers of Europe. The Crusade in itself sounds like a roll-call of the great families of the time. Only the Normans from England, too occupied with the state of affairs in that island, were unrepresented other than by the Duke of Norfolk who was in any case an exile in Brittany.

The first of the nobles to arrive in Constantinople had been Hugh, Count of Vermandois, son of King Henry I of France. Having survived shipwreck on the Greek coast near Dyrrachium, he had been court-eously treated by the Emperor, but had been nevertheless kept in a state of semi-imprisonment. He was, as it were, the test case by which Alexius was determined to show that all the leaders of the expedition must take an oath of fealty to him, and guarantee that they would regard him as their overlord. This meant that, whatever cities or territories the

Opposite: *The Catapult was an effective weapon against castles under siege: from a thirteenth-century manuscript.*

Overleaf: *Krac des Chevaliers in Syria.*

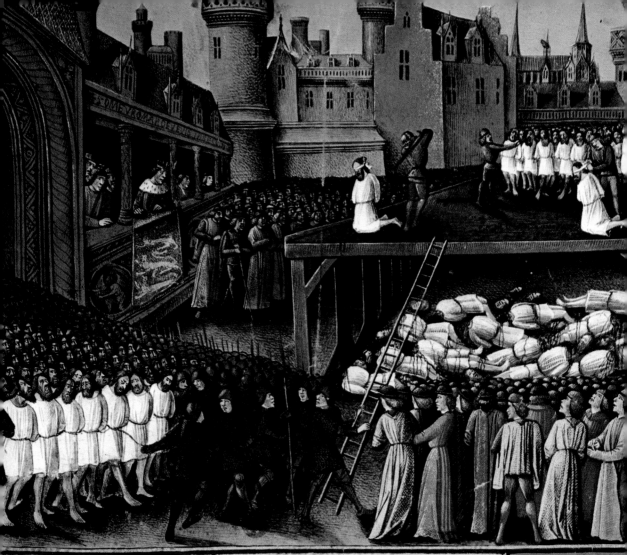

Richart roy dangle
tevre estant de
monte en auve be
ant apres le dept
du roy phelippe le
iour estre venu que salhadm
deuoit rendre la brave trow
et ne lauoit fait. Non obstat
quil eust eu de lui et du roy
phle plusieurs alongemens
pour ce faire fut tant pre
quil fit trencher les testes
a plus de b.ᵐ turcys et auts
sarrazms quil tenoit prisō
niers et le demourant des
autres mist a kaenoon. Et
toft apres sesmeuft grant
dissenoon entre sui et le duc
dosteriche. pour quoy il fit
retter en fange o boe la bame

Crusaders might liberate they would automatically revert to the Emperor. Hugh of Vermandois, a relatively unimportant figure in terms of wealth and territory, was happy to take the oath and receive the Emperor's favour. He had set the precedent, but not all of those who followed behind him would be so willing to acknowledge Alexius as their overlord.

Godfrey of Bouillon, for instance, whose feudal lord was the Emperor of Germany, maintained that for this reason he could not possibly acknowledge Alexius as his suzerain. (It was probably because of his position in relation to the Emperor, that Godfrey had decided on the Hungarian route rather than passing through Italy). It was not long before relations between Godfrey and Alexius reached such a pitch that the Emperor ceased to provide Godfrey's troops, who were camped outside the city, with food and supplies. Things reached a climax when Godfrey, having permitted his troops to loot the suburb of Pera on the northern side of the Golden Horn, crossed over and drew them up in preparation, or so it appeared, for an attack on the palace quarter of Blachernae. Hugh of Vermandois, who had already been used as an emissary by Alexius, was again sent to Godfrey of Bouillon to plead with him to accept the Emperor's terms. Godfrey was disgusted with this Norman who had accepted a Greek, even if an Emperor, as his overlord and dismissed him. Next, over-confident in the capabilities of his troops, he attacked the walls of Constantinople. He found, as many had done before him, that they were virtually impregnable and that the Byzantine troops were well-disciplined and faithful to the Emperor. Disillusioned, but determined not to waste any more men (whom he would certainly need to further his ambitions in the East), Godfrey took the oath of allegiance. At the same time he stipulated that he wanted his troops transported across the Bosporus as quickly as possible. This was as acceptable to the Emperor as it was to the Norman. Alexius knew that further armies were approaching and he had no wish to come under siege by the combined forces of the West.

Throughout this period, when the potentially hostile Norman leaders were arriving outside Constantinople, Alexius managed to secure his position by diplomacy and *savoir-faire*. The fact was that many of these unlettered knights and barons were instinctively suspicious of the whole atmosphere of Constantinople. The comfort and elegance, the evidence of a civilization so infinitely superior to their own, produced a feeling of

Opposite: *Richard the Lion Heart watches the massacre of the Moslem garrison of Acre in 1191 : from* Livres des Passages d'Outremer, *fifteenth-century.*

inferiority. The carefully conducted ceremonial, the ritual almost, of the Byzantine court was something which they had never encountered before. More than that, the splendour of the city, its magnificent palaces, private houses, places of public entertainment, baths and Roman sanitation, reminded them only too forcibly of the poverty and insanitary conditions of the towns and cities that they knew in their own countries.

It is to the credit of Alexius, and of Godfrey and Baldwin (who crossed from Asia Minor for the occasion), that the swearing of fealty to the Byzantine Emperor by the other leaders passed off successfully, with only minor incidents of chauvinism and rudeness to mar the ceremony. With a sigh of relief, no doubt, Alexius finally witnessed them all transferred by the imperial navy to the Asian shore. Here they set up camp, together with those who had preceded them, not far from Cibotos where the crusade of Peter had come to grief. The Emperor now awaited with some concern the arrival of Bohemund of Taranto and the papal legate, Adhemar. Both Bohemund and his father had campaigned against the Byzantines, and it was only eleven years before that Bohemund had himself invaded the Emperor's western territories. Curiously enough, he made no difficulty about acknowledging the suzerainty of Alexius. He had clearly come to the conclusion that the best thing he could do was to make himself the Emperor's right-hand man. At a later date, if all went well and he founded a principality in the East, he could come to his own decision as to his relations with Constantinople. For the moment, however, he suggested that he might be made the Emperor's commander-in-chief in Asia. This was something to which Alexius was very naturally unwilling to accede. It would give this Norman ex-enemy a position of far too much power within the framework of Byzantine policy. He loaded Bohemund with gifts, expressed his complete trust in him, but maintained that such things must wait. In due course, he said, after the success of the Crusade and the return of the Byzantine territories, something on the lines suggested by Bohemund might be worked out. The latter had to content himself with this vague promise. He wanted in any case to keep in good standing with Alexius. More intelligent than many of the other leaders, he saw the necessity of having a friendly Constantinople behind him as well as active cooperation with the Byzantine army and fleet. Robert of Normandy, the last of the principal leaders to arrive, also followed the example of his predecessors and swore allegiance to the Emperor.

The forces of the First Crusade were now assembled on the Asian shore. Only Bohemund's nephew, Tancred, and his cousin, Richard of

Salerno, who had made their way secretly to the Crusaders' camp, had
managed to avoid the oath of fealty completely. All the others had taken
it and even Raymond of Toulouse (who had not pledged himself the
Emperor's man) had at any rate sworn allegiance to defend all Alexius's
interests. The latter, while keeping a keen eye on forthcoming events,
could afford to relax slightly. The marble and gold city of Constantinople, its courtiers, priests, merchants, and even men-at-arms, could
equally relax and wait in expectancy for good news out of the East. They
had seen for themselves that this was no poverty-stricken rabble like its
forerunner. They had seen the shining armoured wave that was soon to
burst over the East.

*Crusader knight pursued by mounted Saracens:
from a thirteenth-century manuscript.*

The Road to Jerusalem

The ancient city of Nicaea, lying not very far from the Sea of Marmora, was the Crusaders' first objective. Nicaea had to be taken to ensure that their communications with Constantinople were not interrupted, and that they had no enemy at their backs when they turned southward for their long trek through Asia Minor. It was an opportune moment to attack, for the Seljuk Sultan, Kilij Arslan, was away putting down a revolt in the eastern region of Sivas, a long distance from his capital. The news that more Franks had landed did not unduly disturb him. He had already seen the bedraggled followers of Peter the Hermit ignominiously defeated, and he had no reason to suspect that this second army of adventurers was any more formidable than the first. By the time the news reached him that Nicaea had been besieged by a large army, and that Alexius was not only supplying the Crusaders with provisions but had also sent up a siege train to assist them, it was too late. When he arrived, he found the city completely invested and, despite his attempt to break through the Crusading ring, he was driven off. Abandoning Nicaea to its fate, he decided to take to the hills and preserve his forces for another day.

In this first major clash of the war one thing became abundantly clear: in a flat open terrain such as that around the city the armoured knights and their men were more than a match for the Turks. Surprise, speed, and mobility were the advantages that the Seljuks had over the Crusaders. In the warfare between Europeans and Turks, and later between Europeans and Arabs, one is inevitably reminded of the ancient gladiatorial combats in imperial Rome between the *Retiarius* and the *Secutor*. The *Retiarius*, like the Moslem, went unarmoured into action, wearing

Opposite: *Knights of the First Crusade : carving on a capital in the church of Notre Dame de Port in Clermont.*

53

only a short apron, and seeking to entangle his opponent in his net and despatch him with his trident as he lay helpless on the ground. The armoured *Secutor*, on the other hand, with his helmet, shield, and sword, had to fight at close quarters. Over the centuries, in the warfare between Crusaders and Moslems, a somewhat similar pattern repeats itself time and again.

Alexius, watching over the campaign from near-by Pelecanum, was pleased with the way it was going. But he was equally determined that the city of Nicaea should be seen to fall to Byzantium, and not be ransacked, looted, and its defences destroyed by the Latins. Accordingly, he entered into communication with the besieged Turks, promising them honourable treatment and assuring them that, if they surrendered to him, he would ensure that it was his own imperial troops, and not the Franks, who entered the city first. For a time the Turks demurred and then, seeing that a general assault was imminent on 19 June, they decided to lay down their arms to the Emperor and the Byzantines whom they knew, rather than to these unknown and uncouth Latins.

When the Crusaders prepared to attack at dawn the following morning they saw to their surprise that the Emperor's standard was already flying over the city walls. Byzantine troops had occupied the city during the night. It was a *fait accompli*, and a most unpopular one with the rank and file of the Crusading army, who felt themselves robbed of the treasures that they had hoped to seize during the sack of the city. This never happened. On the contrary, everything was conducted in an orderly fashion. The Crusaders were only permitted to enter Nicaea in small groups, and then only under the escort of Byzantine troops. Alexius, however, was not so unintelligent as to deny his allies a reasonable taste of the fruits of victory. The soldiers were given presents of food and wine, while their leaders received gold and jewels according to their rank. Alexius's generous treatment of the Turkish captives, however, was far from popular with the Crusaders. The most important Turks were allowed to buy their freedom, and the daughter of the Emir was received in Constantinople with all the honours due to her rank. Alexius, a kindly man by nature, was also astute: if things should go wrong at a later date he wanted the Seljuks to remember that he had treated them with all the honourable courtesies of war.

'Who', writes the author of *Gesta Francorum*, 'is so wise that he can afford to decry the skill, the warlike gifts and the valour of the Turks? Indeed they claim that none but the Franks and themselves have the right to call themselves knights. Certainly if they kept the faith of Christ, they would have no equal in power, in courage and in the science of war.' The Turks for their part, from the time of the First Crusade onwards, had a healthy respect for their Christian adversaries. As one Turkish chronicler was later to write about the Order of St John, that great militant and hospitaller organisation that sprang out of the First Crusade: 'They are good corsairs; they are *men*; and as such they behave . . . Were they not Cross-Kissing Christians, and so much our enemies as they are, they would be very worthy of our esteem; nay, the best of us would take a pride in calling them brothers, and even in fighting under their command.' This early mutual respect was won during the campaign that proceeded as the Crusaders advanced through Asia Minor.

It was clear that only a pitched battle could determine whether the Crusaders were to prosecute their advance southward, or whether the Turk was to retain the vast areas of land that he had won by conquest from Byzantium. The issue was largely decided on a plain outside Dorylaeum, the modern Eskishehr, where Kilij Arslan, having concluded an agreement with the Danishmend Emir with whom he had been fighting, was waiting with his combined forces. On the morning of 1 July, the Turks swooped down from the hills that converged upon the road the Crusaders were taking. They fell upon Bohemund's division which was in advance of the others. The normal tactics of the time were pursued by the Christians, who pitched camp while the mounted knights surrounded it in ordered formation. In Europe this would inevitably have meant a straightforward conflict between two parties of heavy cavalry, but the Turks had evolved their own kind of warfare, one that had given them their supremacy in the East. They circled the camp in much the same manner as the Indians of America would do centuries later against the advancing American pioneers, refused to be drawn into a pitched battle, and poured a storm of arrows into the tents and their defenders. 'Such a [method of] warfare was quite unknown to us', wrote Fulcher of Chartres who was present throughout the engagement.

So long as the contest was fought in this way the advantage was all with the Turks but when, thinking they had sufficiently softened up the enemy, they came to close quarters, they found that the footmen with their pikes and the armoured cavalry were more than a match for them. Meantime a messenger despatched by Bohemund had reached the army that was following. The Turks were dismayed as column after column of cavalry came up at a gallop, Robert of Normandy and Stephen of Blois forming up on the left wing of Bohemund, and Godfrey de Bouillon and Hugh de Vermandois supporting him on the right. Meanwhile Adhemar, Bishop of Puy, a fighting Bishop if ever there was one, had found a track leading off to the left of the battle. Having led his troops along this, screened from observation by a low foothill, he brought them out in the rear of the Turks. The battle was as good as over. Sultan Kilij had already lost his principal city of Nicaea, and he was now to lose his camp and all its treasures. The Turk, ever a nomad at heart, tended to travel with most of his valuable possessions, and the loss of the Sultan's camp was far from being just the loss of a tented, fortified position. The loot acquired from the Sultan's tent somewhat compensated the Crusaders for what they had failed to gain at Nicaea.

Dorylaeum was an important battle in the history of warfare. The Turks, who had long ago crushed the Arabs and Byzantines, found themselves up against something new and formidable in the lines of armoured men. Dorylaeum proved that, if only the knights were to hold their ground in formation until the moment served for attack, they were more than a match for their enemy. It is noteworthy that the only tactical reverse occurred when a knight, who had already distinguished himself by his aggressiveness in Constantinople, led a charge against the Turks – contrary to Raymond's orders – and was beaten back with his followers under a hail of Turkish arrows. The day of individual charges, so important a feature of the chivalric conception of warfare, was over. The armoured mass, containing itself until the harassing tactics of the enemy had spent themselves, and then going into action when the archers had depleted themselves of arrows, was to prove the decisive weapon against the Turk in the field. The method was somewhat akin to the British 'square' (so important a feature of colonial warfare in the nineteenth century), where the disciplined troops, having contained themselves and their firepower under a hail of spears and arrows, outsat the storm and then took their revenge upon an enemy whose weaponry was exhausted.

After resting two days at Dorylaeum the army struck south again, crossing the Anatolian plateau to reach Pisidian Antioch (made memorable centuries before by the visit of St Paul), and thence on to Iconium. In the heat of summer the men and their animals suffered severely, the Turks having destroyed or fouled as many of the wells and waterholes as they could. As they approached Heraclea, whose fertile valley promised them respite and water for men and beasts, they found a Turkish army drawn up against them under the command of two Emirs from Cappadocia, both of whom were anxious to prevent the Crusaders passing through their territory. They hoped to force them down to the coast, to take the southern route through the Taurus mountains into Syria. The leaders of the Crusade were most unwilling to cross the

Taurus range, something that could only be done by passing through the Cilician Gates, one of the longest and most difficult passes in the world. Bohemund, determined that the way should be made clear for the army's progress through Cappadocia and right through the north into Syria, formed up the cavalry and charged. The Turks, remembering what had happened at Dorylaeum, dispersed and withdrew. They had learned their lesson quickly.

After their victory at Heraclea the main body of the army turned to the northeast towards Caesarea, hoping among other things to establish friendly contacts with the local Armenian princes who were hostile to the Turks. A smaller sub-division, lead by Tancred and Godfrey's brother Baldwin, elected to head south – risking the Cilician Gates – in an attempt to capture Tarsus and establish a hold on the area of Cilicia. Already it is easy to see that the process of carving up small personal principalities by the leaders had begun to disturb the overall purpose of the Crusade. Tancred and Baldwin were to fall out over the possession

Crusaders pitch camp: detail from a twelfth-century manuscript.

of Tarsus, to such an extent that at one moment a skirmish even took place between the rival bands of Crusaders. This diversion to the south laid the seeds of what was later to be part of the Christian principality of Antioch.

Throughout the advance of the army of the First Crusade through Asia it is noteworthy that the Crusaders handed over the possession of every captured city to Byzantine administrators and delegates. Alexius meanwhile, after refortifying Nicaea, was busily engaged in re-establishing Byzantine control over the vast territories left behind. One of his principal objectives was to reopen the road from Nicaea to Dorylaeum, southward to Smyrna and along the coast to Ephesus, at the same time as his fleet recaptured the coastal towns and the off-lying Aegean islands. His aim was to establish a secure route whence the Crusaders, as soon as they had entered Syria, could be reinforced by both land and sea. Despite complaints by the Latins about the duplicity of the Byzantines, it would seem that the Emperor attempted to keep his side of the bargain.

The main body of the army under Bohemund passed without much event through Cappadocia. At Marash, half way between Caesarea and Antioch, Baldwin rejoined the main body. He was not to stay with it for long, for Baldwin was consumed with his own ambitions. The liberation of Jerusalem meant far less to him than the establishment of an independent kingdom, and his interest lay to the east in the city of Edessa. His former breakaway partner Tancred, having captured Alexandretta, crossed the Amanus range into Syria and joined the army when it was encamped before Antioch. The diversion of these two bodies of Crusaders to the south, even if both of them were only motivated by private cupidity, had at least served some purpose in establishing a hold, however limited, over Cilicia. This might serve to prevent the Turks moving in from the west, and interfering with the Christian operations in Syria.

The capture of Antioch was all-important at this stage. The ancient city had once been the third greatest in the Roman Empire. It was here that Antony and Cleopatra had once passed a winter, and here that St Paul had astonished the congregation with accounts of his proselytising in Asia Minor and Greece. It had declined under the Arabs, and the capital of Syria was now established at Damascus. Nevertheless, Antioch still presented the key to Syria and the south. Captured by the Turks from the Byzantines in the tenth century, it was at this moment to all intents and purposes ruled by the Turkish Yaghi-Siyan. Yaghi-Siyan was not fortunate in his subjects. Most of them were Christians, an uneasy mixture of Syrians, Armenians, and Orthodox Greeks, nearly all of whom disliked one another intensely.

The army of the First Crusade encamped before the walls of Antioch in late October 1097. Such confidence as they may have acquired during their successful march through Turkish Asia Minor tended to fade away when they saw the walls of Antioch. Lying on a plain, the city was about two and a half miles long from east to west and a mile from north to south. To the north it was defended by the river Orontes while to the south Mount Silpius, which had been the site of the citadel since classical times, defended the city, barring the road beyond it and any attempt to take Antioch from the rear. Four hundred towers guarded the city's walls, each designed to be within bowshot of the other.

The city, ably fortified by the great Byzantine Emperor Justinian centuries before, and brought up to date by military architects in

Godfrey de Bouillon in a siege-tower : from Romans de Godefroi de Bouillon et de Salehadin, *a fourteenth-century French manuscript.*

comparatively recent times, presented a formidable front to any attacking army. And the soldiers of the First Crusade had not been able to
bring with them a cumbrous 'tail' of heavy siege equipment during their
long march through Asia Minor. Raymond, for his part, was all for a
straightforward frontal assault, trusting in their courage and in their
faith to lead them to victory. He was overruled by more cautious advisers.
Bohemund counselled that they should proceed slowly, wait for siege
engines, and – as he really trusted – attempt to take the city by treachery
from within the walls. He himself had his eyes on Antioch as a personal
possession, as the capital from which he might administer a rich principality. On the face of it his more prudent counsel may have seemed wise.
In fact, so great was the reputation already earned by the Crusaders and
so impoverished in numbers were the defenders (they could not man
the circle of the walls), that Antioch would probably have yielded to the
first determined assault.

Winter succeeded autumn and still the encamped Crusaders and the
besieged Antiochenes watched one another uneasily. There were spies
in both camps. The most important event for the Crusaders during this
time of waiting was the arrival of a Genoese squadron at Antioch's main
port, St Simeon, bringing reinforcements of men and arms. This was
a much-needed boost to morale, but the principal problem that confronted the army was that of food. They had found the country around
Antioch well supplied with grain and with plenty of flocks when they
had marched down. But in medieval armies commissariat matters were
hardly understood at all. At home in Europe the campaigning season
came to an end with the beginning of winter; during the summer and
autumn months the troops mainly lived off the land. Everything was
different in this campaign, carried out so far from home, in an unfamiliar
climate and terrain. By Christmas 1097 the army was so seriously short
of food that it was decided to send Bohemund with a force of some 20,000
men down the Orontes valley in the direction of Hama, to collect what
food they could from the villages *en route*. During his absence, which
could hardly be concealed even if Yaghi-Siyan had not learned about it
from agents in the camp, the Turks launched a sudden night attack on
the depleted Christian forces. Despite the benefit to them of initial
surprise, Raymond of Toulouse rallied his men, counter-attacked and,
but for confusion in the darkness, very nearly succeeded in following
the fleeing Turks through the city gates. This in itself seems evidence
enough that, if Raymond's original plan of immediate attack on Antioch
had been followed, the city would have been taken with comparative
ease.

Bohemund meanwhile had run into the forces of the Emir Duqaq of

Damascus who was marching north to the relief of Antioch. Despite an initial setback, when Robert of Normandy's troops in the van were nearly cut off, the Moslems were routed in a spirited charge led by Bohemund. Once again it was seen that under the right conditions the horsemen of Europe were more than a match for the enemy. Losses were serious, however, and Bohemund was forced to make his way back to Antioch without the supplies and provisions which had been the whole object of the sortie. The situation was now nearly desperate for the Crusaders, with famine threatening and morale at a very low ebb. At this point Bishop Adhemar asserted his religious authority, ordered a three-day fast (scarcely necessary) and, having reproached the troops for their behaviour to the local inhabitants, had all camp-followers and prostitutes driven out of the camp. Adultery was declared punishable by death; and drinking, gambling and swearing were strictly forbidden. Whether these ecclesiastical moves had any effect on the army's morale remains doubtful. Indeed, so deep was the despair that deserters became plentiful, among them astonishingly enough being Peter the Hermit. Captured and brought back in ignomity, Peter, whose reputation had in any case been discredited since the failure of the People's

The Attack on Antioch. In June 1098 Antioch fell to the Crusaders: from William of Tyre's History, c.1280.

61

Crusade, was pardoned. He was yet to have an opportunity to prove himself.

A further threat developed early in 1098 when Ridwan, King of Aleppo, made a move to relieve Antioch. Once again superior tactics and the weight of the Crusader cavalry charge turned the tide, Ridwan and his forces being routed. In this as in the previous action, it was Bohemund who was the hero of the hour. Throughout the whole conduct of the operations in front of Antioch, Bohemund stands out as the leader *par excellence*. The main reason probably lay in the fact that at no time did he lose sight of his main objective – a principality with Antioch its capital. At one moment during the lowest ebb of the Crusaders' fortunes he had even threatened to leave and take his men with him, pleading that he could not afford the cost of operations any longer. It was only when the other barons promised that Antioch should be his if he would stay that he relented. Bohemund was not only an excellent soldier but a wily politician. He knew well enough that the Crusade would practically collapse if he withdrew. He now had the guarantee that he needed.

Early in March a fleet commanded by Edgar Atheling, former pretender to the English throne and grand-nephew of Edward the Confessor, put into St Simeon. The fleet had many pilgrims among its passengers, but what was far more important, it contained a large quantity of siege material and mechanics to construct siege engines and operate them. These had been put aboard when the fleet had called at Constantinople. Once again Alexius had not failed the Crusaders and, however much they might complain later about Byzantine sharp-practice, the Emperor had fulfilled his side of the bargain. At this particular stage the arrival of men and material was vital, for it was known that further attempts were being made to relieve Antioch and that the Lord of Mosul among others was marching south into Syria. It was clear that with the materials for siege engines and towers to overtop the walls now in their hands they must take the city before the threatened relief force arrived.

With the aid of these towers, as well as a small castle, known as 'The Castle of Raymond', the encirclement of the city was almost complete by the end of March. But it was not until 3 June, 1098, that Antioch finally fell to the Crusaders. Its capture came only just in time, for the relief force under Kerboqa, the Sultan of Mosul, was not more than a few days' march away. That the city fell so conveniently at this moment was almost entirely due to the activities of Bohemund. He had for a long time been in contact with dissidents within the walls, among them one of Yaghi-Siyan's commanders, an Armenian called Firuz. The latter was in command of some all-important towers in the city's defences, which guarded the Gate of St George. Firuz was a Moslem-convert but he may have had some sentiment towards his former co-religionists, as well as some private scores to settle in the city. Bohemund was determined that it should be by treachery that Antioch should fall, rather than by a more conventional assault in which his rival Raymond of Toulouse might achieve distinction, and possibly manage to ensure the support of the other leaders so that the city should not be solely the prize of Bohemund.

Yaghi-Siyan was not surprised when, on the evening of 2 June, he saw the main body of the Crusader army breaking camp and striking out eastward. He knew that help in the person of the Sultan of Mosul and his troops was not far away. It seemed clear that the enemy was marching out to meet him. The ruse had been devised by Bohemund who had received the news from his Armenian accomplice that Antioch would be betrayed that night. After dark, while the army was silently marching back to take up its positions, Bohemund and a small band of sixty men scaled the walls by a rope let down from above, to which was attached a ladder. Bohemund was the first to mount the wall. As he reached the top, a hand seized his and a voice hissed: 'Long live this hand'.

The towers guarding the gate were silently taken and at daybreak, reinforced by further Crusaders and by Christian sympathisers in the city, the Gate of St George was opened, as well as the Gate of the

Left: *siege warfare : early fourteenth century manuscript.*
Right: *Crusaders and Saracens meet in battle : thirteenth century.*

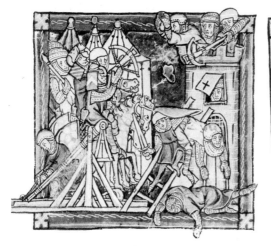 

Mounted Saracens (left) *and Crusaders in a galley loaded with crossbows : from*
A Handbook for Crusaders by *Marinus Sanutus, c. 1321.*

Bridge, outside which the main body of the army was massed. Such Turks as survived the main avalanche of men as they swept into the city took refuge in the citadel. The scenes that followed were prophetic of others yet to come in Crusader history. The city was abandoned to the mindless rape, loot and murder inflicted by half-starving men who took their pleasure and their pay with the sword.

Yaghi-Siyan had fled during the chaos and confusion. He had gallantly defended Antioch for seven months and, had he been able to hold out for a few days more, the city would undoubtedly have been relieved by the advancing army of the Sultan. During his flight into the mountains Yaghi-Siyan was thrown from his horse and left for dead by his escort. Some Armenians who were working nearby recognised the body and cut off his head. They brought it to Bohemund and were handsomely rewarded. Thus, despite the fact that the citadel was still in the hands of Turks under the command of a son of Yaghi-Siyan, Antioch had finally fallen in the first major siege of the Crusade. If Alexius could have been present he would have received every confirmation of his wisdom in making sure that Nicaea had fallen into his hands and not into those of his allies. The *furor Normanorum*, which was later to burst over other walls and other cities, had its way with Antioch. By evening the city which the Romans had called Antioch the Golden was no more. Amid the smouldering, blood-stained ruins of its houses the soldiers of the First Crusade were as busy as jackals.

The Spear of Antioch

The Crusaders were not to enjoy the fruits of their victory for long. Only three days after the capture of Antioch the army of Sultan Kerboqa reached the Iron Bridge, where the roads from Aleppo and Marash joined to cross the river Orontes. They were only three hours march from the city. The absence of any discipline, which bedevilled armies in the Middle Ages during the period when a captured city was turned over to the soldiers to loot, was to have fearsome repercussions upon the soldiers of the First Crusade. During the three days' grace before the arrival of the Sultan they had done little or nothing to obtain provisions from the countryside. This was already ravaged by their locust-like occupation during the siege, while Antioch itself, after its seven-month ordeal, was practically bare of provisions. The only constructive action seems to have been to wall off the Turkish-held citadel. Even so, when Kerboqa took it over from Yaghi-Siyan's son, it was only with difficulty that the Crusaders managed to prevent his troops flooding over the wall and pouring into the city itself.

Knowing well enough that Antioch had been on the verge of starvation even before the Christians had captured it, and that their position was desperate, Kerboqa settled down to encircle the city and reduce Antioch by starvation. In the days that followed, as William of Tyre wrote, 'Anyone who found even a dead dog or cat was more than happy to eat it'. It looked for a time as if this was to be the end of the whole expedition, and it was hardly surprising that there were a number of deserters. Some of them, slipping through the Turkish lines by night, made their way to St Simeon and told the sailors aboard the ships there that Antioch was doomed.

Opposite: *Godfrey de Bouillon cuts off a camel's head: from* Romans de Godefroi de Bouillon et de Salehadin, *a fourteenth-century manuscript.*

Many of the ships in harbour put to sea, the deserters embarking with them, and made their way to the Port of Tarsus. The only hope, so it seemed to the besieged in Antioch, was that the Emperor Alexius, who was known to have set out from Constantinople in the spring, might come to their rescue. But by this time Alexius, who had heard of the army's plight, had reached the conclusion that he could not proceed any farther through Asia Minor. Were he to do so he would risk not only his army but his whole Empire by over-extending his lines of communication. He made the practical decision to withdraw, and consolidate his position throughout the parts of the Empire that had already been recaptured. All this the Crusaders, locked up in their starving city, were not to know. All they did know was that day by day things grew worse and the likelihood that they would have to capitulate drew nearer. After their massacre of the Turks and other Moslems in Antioch they can have had little hope for their own fate. Throughout this period of starvation, sickness, and strain, Bohemund moved like a giant – ensuring that positions were manned as far as possible, and rallying the dispirited by his presence and his determination. Even so there can be no doubt that Antioch would have been lost but for an extraordinary, and seemingly miraculous, event.

Knowing the complete faith that was placed in relics during this period it is perhaps not so surprising that it was the discovery in Antioch of a relic of a value beyond all others previously known to the West that turned the despair of the Crusaders into a blinding conviction that they must triumph. Never perhaps in history has the morale of an apparently ruined army been revived so quickly. A Provençal peasant of somewhat dubious character, named Peter Bartholomew, sought an audience of Raymond of Toulouse and Bishop Adhemar. He told them that he had had recurrent visions of St Andrew, in which the Saint had told him that under the church of St Peter in Antioch there lay a relic of priceless virtue – the lance with which the Roman soldier had pierced the side of Christ when he was dying on the Cross. Adhemar tended to be somewhat sceptical about the whole matter, but further signs and portents – a priest called Peter testifying to a vision of Christ, and a meteor which seemed to the defenders of Antioch to fall upon the place where the Turks were encamped – contrived to induce an astounding spirit of belief. Permission was finally given for a gang of workmen to start excavating the floor of the church. A whole day went by and still nothing had been discovered. Then Peter himself jumped into the excavation. He seized something which he held up, commanding all those present to kneel in prayer. In his hand was a piece of iron, a nail say some, others a lance-head. (One Moslem commentator surmises that Peter had buried the lance himself.) Whatever views one may take of the whole event there can be no doubt of its effect upon the Crusaders. At the news of the discovery, writes the chronicler of *Gesta Francorum*, 'the whole city was filled with immense joy'.

Meanwhile all was not well in the Moslem confederation that encircled Antioch. Family feuds, and friction between Arabs and Turks (never the happiest of allies), were causing widespread dissension in the investing army. St Andrew, one cannot help suspecting, had some knowledge of the uneasy climate that prevailed among the enemies of the Christians . . . But, rationalise as one may, the fact remains that the discovery of the lance (what purported to be the original was already in Constantinople) had an effect that to a modern seems almost incredible. To a medieval man, who believed implicitly in the efficacy of relics, this piece of iron was almost akin to the Holy Grail. The nervous strength imparted to the starving Crusaders can only be judged in the light of subsequent modern investigations conducted into psychology and the activities of the mind under stress. 'A psychosis superinduced by ideation' is a technical description that might be used to account for the wave of unnatural enthusiasm that now swept the besieged Christians. But this would in no way really explain the metamorphosis from despairing resignation to uncontrollable enthusiasm. Whatever Bishop Adhemar and some others thought about its authenticity, the discovery of the lance changed the whole complexion of affairs. Knights and

An army on the move in Italy: detail from an eleventh-century Italian manuscript in the Benedictine Abbey of Monte Cassino.

soldiers were convinced that Christ was with them, and that they were destined not only to destroy the relieving army but to recapture Jerusalem.

Bohemund was now in overall command of the army. His rival, Count Raymond, was ill and, when the army marched out, was left behind in charge of a small number of men deputed to keep watch on the Turkish-held citadel. The decision had been taken to attack. It was on the morning of 28 June, 1098, that the Crusaders, divided into six regiments or 'battles', began to march out of the city. Prior to this last and desperate move they had tried to negotiate with Kerboqa. Peter the Hermit, being a non-combatant, was chosen as head of the mission. Although he failed to talk Kerboqa into any acceptable terms, it becomes clear that Peter's previous conduct was now forgiven if not forgotten.

The army crossed the Gate of the Bridge, while Kerboqa waited. He restrained his troops until all the Crusaders were out in the open. He hoped to destroy them in one sweeping action, and not to have a large mass of men escaping back into the city, thus compelling him once again to resort to siege tactics. The first of the regiments to cross was

Military training with lances, swords and cross-bows.

composed of northern French and men of Flanders, under the command of Robert of Flanders and Hugh of Vermandois. Next followed the men of Lorraine under Godfrey de Bouillon; then the Normans under William the Conqueror's son, Duke Robert; fourth, the men of Provence under Bishop Adhemar (since Raymond was ill); fifth the Normans from Italy under Tancred; and lastly more Norman-Italians under Bohemund, who was in overall command. The army was not so splendid-looking as it had been in the days when it had first moved into Asia on its way to Nicaea. Many of the knights were compelled to march on foot, some were on shabby half-starved mounts, and the swords and pike-heads that had once gleamed so splendidly were tarnished and dull. Raymond of Aguilers, historian of the Crusade, who claimed that he had touched the lance while it was still embedded in the earth below the church floor, carried the relic into battle.

As soon as all the Crusaders were across the bridge they drew up in line. Then they began a steady advance towards the enemy. The latter attempted to turn the left flank of the army. Kerboqa's aim was to get behind the Christians and secure the bridge, but his men were beaten

From Marinus Sanutus's Handbook for Crusaders, *c.1321*.

back by the rearguard troops under Bohemund. Having feigned a retreat in order to lure the Crusaders out, Kerboqa now found that his stratagem had worked against him. Many of his men had turned what was intended to be an ordered retreat into flight. At the same time, a number of the Emirs supporting him decided that they were not going to risk their troops against this formidable and orderly army that came against them. The Crusaders, for their part, inspired by the lance, and driven on by the desperation of men who knew that to return to Antioch would be to starve, fought like madmen.

Betrayed and deserted by many of his supporters, Kerboqa, after one last attempt to change the course of battle by setting fire to the sun-dried grass between his men and Crusaders, took to his heels. The Moslem commander of the citadel, seeing the army in headlong retreat, hastily despatched a messenger to Raymond to announce his surrender. Antioch was saved, and so was the Crusade.

Opposite: *Chateau Gaillard, France, built by Richard the Lion Heart between 1195 and 1199 : it was eventually captured by Philip Augustus from King John in 1204.*

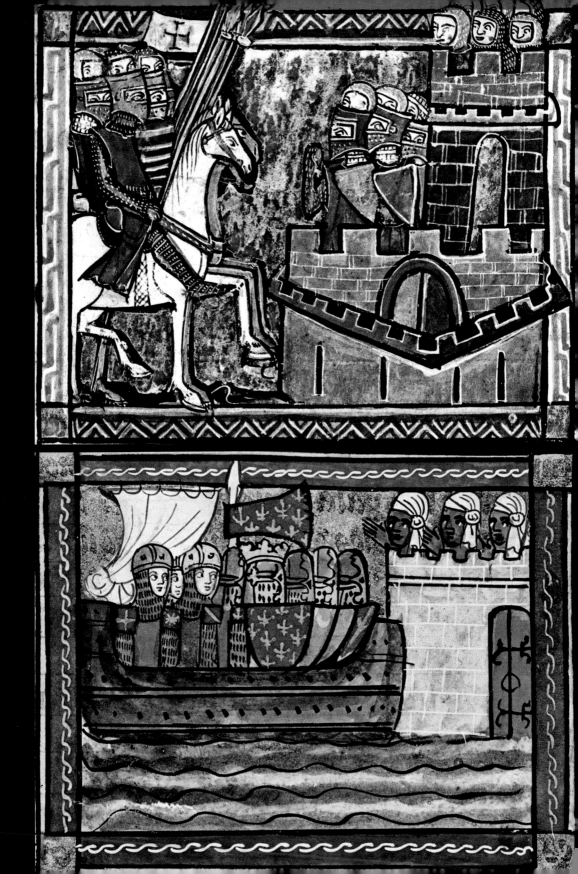

Jerusalem

There could not be, there never had been, any secret as to the ultimate destination of the First Crusade. Even before it had landed in Asia its intentions had been widely known. There had been no secret about Pope Urban's words. In the weeks and months of preparation, during the slow advance through Europe, and then over the lands formerly dominated by the Turks, it had always been clear that the aim of these Franks was to capture Jerusalem. From a practical point of view the Crusaders should now have capitalised on their success at Antioch, and on their high morale resulting not only from this victory but from the certainty that, travelling with the lance, they were destined to conquer. Unfortunately, and it was symptomatic of the disease of personal rivalry that was to be the bane of the Crusades, these advantages were immediately thrown away.

No sooner had Antioch been regained than the leaders of the army began to quarrel amongst themselves as to the ownership of the city, and of the territory that it commanded. Antioch might at the moment be something of a ruin – except for its walls and defences – but it could, and would, once again become one of the greatest cities and emporiums of Syria. Raymond was still ill, Bishop Adhemar was also ill (and destined to die in Antioch), so it seemed that Bohemund would easily be able to gain control. The Crusaders, however, remembering their pledge to

Opposite top: *Mounted Lancers parading before a besieged city, in order to demoralise the enemy.*

Opposite bottom: *Henry VI and his Crusaders approach a Saracen-held fortress by sea: from a fourteenth-century manuscript.*

75

deliver all captured places to the Byzantines – and thinking no doubt that the addition of the Byzantine army would be of immense value in the forthcoming battle for Jerusalem – sent Hugh de Vermandois with a message for the Emperor. They would, they said, hand over Antioch to him, but on the condition that 'he himself come to help us in the siege of Jerusalem'.

While their leaders wrangled, and everyone waited for a reply, the morale of the Crusaders inevitably deteriorated. Far from all of them had left their homes, households and lands for personal gain, let alone to found new principalities in the East. The majority of them, indeed, had quite genuinely taken the Cross with the sole object of delivering Jerusalem. Under these circumstances it was not surprising that the unnecessarily enforced delay caused some to break away into splinter parties: some looting the countryside, and others going north to join Baldwin in Edessa. Others again went to the siege of Maarat-an-Naman, a town to the south of Antioch, the Arab defenders of which courageously resisted their attack, the city finally falling in December 1098. Meanwhile no word had been received from Constantinople (it was not to come until April of the following year) and disease, probably typhoid, had broken out in the captured city. This was hardly surprising, for the Crusaders' notions of hygiene were as rude as those of most men in medieval Europe.

Among the victims was Bishop Adhemar. He was a most serious loss

Baldwin and his Crusaders (left) *receive the surrender of the Armenians and Turks at Edessa in 1099 : from William of Tyre's* History, *c.1280.*

to the Crusade. He, almost alone, had throughout preserved the spirit and the intention of the Pope. He had worked ceaselessly to try and prevent the ambitions of the leaders from destroying the central purpose for which all had joined. He had presided wisely over many councils, and he had also proved himself brave in the field and a good strategist. His death was seen by the whole army as a tragic blow. Their morale was even further reduced. The disputes of their leaders were seen – in stark contrast to the attitude that had been shown by Adhemar – as being little or no different from the same feuds that bedevilled the Europe they had left behind them.

The first to show that his intentions were unchanged was Raymond of Toulouse. He set out barefoot, walking as a Christian pilgrim, at the head of his men, heading south from Maarat-an-Naman. Ostensibly dedicated to the Crusade's objective, Jerusalem, he was also nursing a profound grudge against Bohemund. The latter, for his part, was determined to hold on to Antioch and consolidate his position there. Baldwin continued to look after his interests in Edessa. Of the behaviour of the Crusaders, particularly the nobles, Sir John Glubb has written perspicaciously in his *The Course of Empire*: 'Modern writers have condemned in scathing terms the Crusaders' desire to seize cities and provinces. In fact, however, there is another side to this question. War is a notoriously expensive occupation. The barons had left home carrying bundles of coins, for there were no banks . . . The only way they knew of obtaining money was from land. Thus it may well be argued that the continuance of the campaign against the Muslims made it vital for them to seize land from which they could replenish their finances, an aspect of the situation largely neglected by historians.'

Raymond, quite apart from his envy of Bohemund, was not only setting out southward hoping to be the first at Jerusalem. He too needed land, and the money that went with it. He had his eye on Tripoli, one of the most important ports in the East, and a city surrounded by fair and fertile ground, backed by a chain of mountains. He did in fact relinquish this ambition – for the moment at any rate – when later pressed by the other leaders to go on to Jerusalem. But the thought of Tripoli and its countryside, a principality that would eclipse Bohemund's Antioch, was never far from his mind.

It was not until the middle of May 1099 that the major part of the Crusader army was on the march towards its objective. They knew by now that they could expect no help from Alexius. Although he wrote that he could bring his army down to Syria by July, they felt sure from the long delay in his reply that he could not be relied upon. Had they

known the truth, they would hardly have been surprised, even if con-
firmed in their belief as to the duplicity of the Byzantines. Alexius was,
in fact, in correspondence with the Vizier of Egypt – and it was an
Egyptian army that held Jerusalem. Afdhal, the Vizier, who himself a
Moslem was nonetheless of Christian-Armenian descent, proposed to
the Crusaders that they might visit Jerusalem and the Holy Places, but
only on condition that they came as pilgrims and left their arms behind.
His offer seemed to him perfectly reasonable – as in a sense indeed it
was – but he was not dealing with Byzantines nor with ordinary pilgrims.
The psychology of the warlike Normans for a long time remained incomprehensible to all Moslems. If it was only a question of visiting
places and shrines, then let them come – as they had so often done in the
past. But the matter was far from as simple as that. The pilgrimages of
the past had been superseded by the Crusades which, though still to
some extent pilgrimages, were inspired by militancy.

While Raymond was besieging Arqa, a keypoint town to the north of
Tripoli, Peter Bartholomew, whose vision had led to the discovery of
the lance, infuriated by the many doubts that had been cast upon his
divine inspiration, submitted to the ordeal by fire. Clearly he himself
believed in the truth of what he said, for the ordeal by fire was not to be
lightly undertaken – involving as it did walking through a blazing corridor
on either side of which logs had been set ablaze. In the event, though
Peter did survive for a number of days, he ultimately died of his burns.
The sceptics, the hard-headed Normans who had always mistrusted
Peter's vision (since he was a Provençal and the lance had practically
become a Provençal political possession), could maintain that this proved
that he was an impostor. The believers could point to the fact that he had
not died immediately – as the guilty would have done. To a modern the
episode seems incomprehensible (as it would probably have been to a
Byzantine, great though their faith in relics), but to the superstitious and
illiterate western Europeans such beliefs were part and parcel of their
lives. If a man was innocent, God would not permit him to suffer, and
conversely. The ordeal proved nothing – except possibly that the scepti-
cism of the intelligent Adhemar had been right in the first place. In any
case, that practical Bishop would probably never have permitted the
test to be made had he still been alive.

Raymond very reluctantly abandoned the siege of Arqa at the press-
ing request of the other leaders of the Crusade. Three days later, on
16 May, the army entered the territories of the Emir of Tripoli. Along
with them, as they closed the coast, surged the ships of Genoa, Venice,
France, and England, ready and eager to supply them when the cam-

paign began. The Genoese, whose interests always lay in obtaining trading privileges and special quarters for their merchants in the ports and cities of the East, were determined to be one jump ahead of their hated rivals the Venetians. The ambitions of the latter were identical. One of the most important offshoots of the Crusades was the growth of Italian maritime republics and the widespread development of commercial shipping throughout the eastern Mediterranean. It was not only that the armies in years to come would largely be dependent upon them for their transport, but the opening up of trade with the East, and the number of pilgrims requiring to be taken to and from the Holy Places, all made for an increase in shipbuilding. These factors helped to establish the fortunes of many maritime states from Amalfi in western Italy to Venice in the east.

After concluding an agreement with the Emir of Tripoli, the army marched peacefully through the delightful country of the Lebanon,

William, Archbishop of Tyre, a Crusade Historian

swaying with vines and olives in rich acres of well-cultivated land. They forgot the Tenth Commandment as they looked about them, for everything was an invitation to future conquest and appropriation. From Beirut to Sidon and south to Tyre, although all were Egyptian-occupied, the army passed practically unscathed. But the messages meanwhile were winging by pigeon throughout the whole area, calling upon the Moslems to prepare to rise against the invader. The fleet was now no longer able to supply them, because all the ports were held by the Egyptians, with the result that the army was forced to live off the land. After leaving Caesarea and Arsuf, they swung inland towards the Moslem town of Ramlah, which they found deserted by its inhabitants. Every day was taking them nearer to their goal.

They were heartened above all when the inhabitants of Bethlehem came out to meet them, begging to be freed from the Moslem yoke, and Tancred in company with Baldwin and his men made a diversion to the birthplace of Christ. A very heartening event was an eclipse of the moon foretelling, as they believed, the imminent eclipse of the Crescent. On the day after this, the first Crusaders, passing to the east of the tomb of the Prophet Samuel, came to the summit of the road where it crossed the hilltop that earlier pilgrims had named Mount Joy. It was the morning of 7 June, 1099, when the cry went up, to be echoed down the lines, 'Jerusalem!'

In view of subsequent events it is important to realise just what this sight meant to these simple but battle-hardened men. William of Tyre's description graphically portrays the scene: 'When they heard the name Jerusalem called out, they began to weep and fell on their knees, giving thanks to Our Lord with many sighs for the great love which He had shown them in allowing them to reach the goal of their pilgrimage, the Holy City which He had loved so much that He wished there to save the world. It was deeply moving to see the tears and hear the loud sobs of these good people. They ran forward until they had a clear view of all the towers and walls of the city. Then they raised their hands in prayers to Heaven and, taking off their shoes, bowed to the ground and kissed the earth.'

Jerusalem at this time was one of the most strongly fortified cities in the world. Built on a narrow spur of the mountains, with a ravine to east and west, it could only be attacked from north or south and, although a foothold was possible on Mount Zion to the south, it was hardly suitable for an assault of any proportions. Only to the north was there an open flat area running up to the city walls, between the Gate of Damascus and the Gate of Herod. The walls themselves were formidable.

The taking of Jerusalem in 1099 by the Crusaders : from a French mid-fourteenth-century edition of William of Tyre's History.

Ever since the capture of Jerusalem by the Romans in the reign of the Emperor Hadrian its defences had been continually improved, and later by the Byzantines and the Moslems. The defence of the city was in the hands of the governor, Iftikhar-ad-Dowla, who had already taken the precaution of filling in, or poisoning, all the wells outside the city walls. It seemed likely that if the siege of Antioch had taken seven months the siege of Jerusalem would take even more.

The Crusaders' first attempt on the walls, on 13 June, was frustrated by the fact that there were not enough scaling ladders to hand, and the garrison was courageous and determined. In the high Judaean summer men and beasts alike began to suffer from shortage of water and provisions. Parties sent out to neighbouring springs some six miles away were cut down by troops sent by the garrison to ambush them, while foraging parties met a similar fate. It seemed clear that the siege to be successful must be a quick one, for the harsh terrain outside Jerusalem offered little or nothing for an invader. As at Antioch, the Crusaders

The siege of Jerusalem in 1099 by a vast encampment of Crusaders: from a mid-fifteenth-century manuscript.

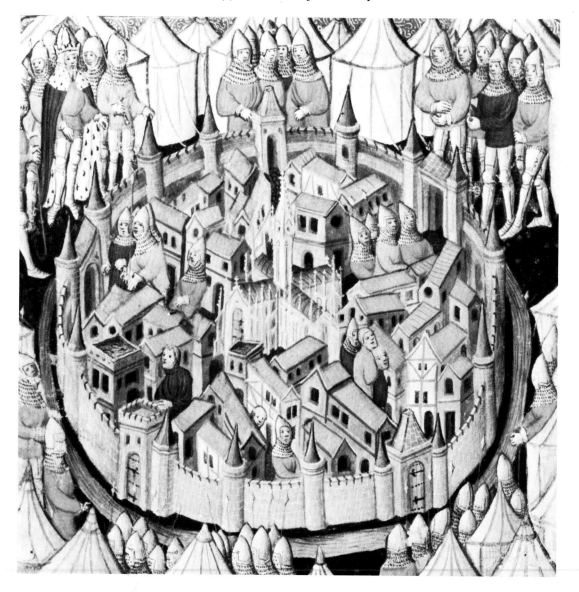

were largely saved by the arrival of ships. Six merchantmen put in at Jaffa, a city that should have been in Moslem hands but from which the defenders seem to have fled after the passage of the army. Genoese and English vessels, which had brought not only supplies but most important of all wood, nails and materials for constructing siege-engines and towers, now began to unload their cargoes, the sailors transporting the food and essential materials up to the waiting army. The leaders of the Crusade were now well aware that time was not on their side. Report had reached them that, in answer to the governor's appeals, a large army was on its way from Egypt to relieve Jerusalem.

In the midst of all this activity – blacksmiths and carpenters busy on the frames of the engines, and men and women stitching together the

Plan of Jerusalem drawn in c.1170.

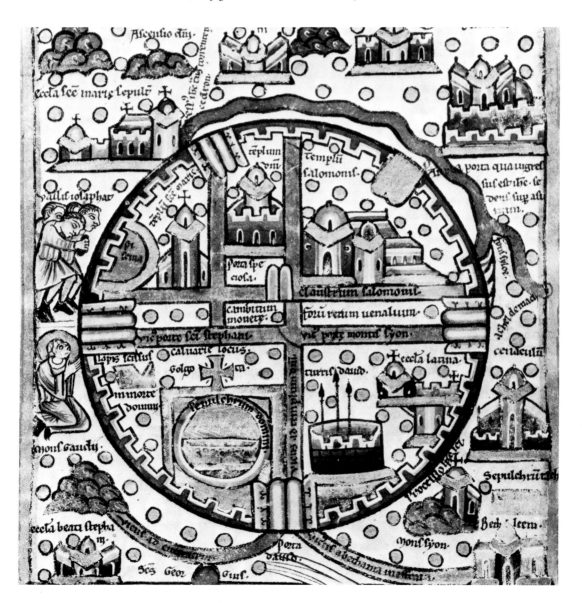

hides of beasts to protect the wood against the Greek fire and flaming missiles of the defenders – the religious aspect was not forgotten. On Friday, 8 July, a solemn fast was observed throughout the army. Chaplains and preachers, among them Peter the Hermit, addressed the assembled throng, and a procession set out around the walls of the city. All walked barefoot. While the enemy mocked them, the Crusaders consecrated themselves to the liberation of the Holy City. Within a day they had begun to move up the hastily assembled siege-engine and towers, Godfrey de Bouillon being in overall charge of one tower and Robert of Normandy of another. The main attack was to be directed against the north wall, while a secondary attack and bombardment were carried out from Mount Zion. At the time of the attack on Jerusalem the army's strength, according to Raymond de Aguilers, was 12,000 foot soldiers and 1200 knights. Apart from these, there were many pilgrims and men, women and children, as well as the inevitable camp-followers hanging like jackals around lions waiting for the kill.

At dawn on 14 July, with the great siege engines hurling their rocks against the ancient walls, and the defenders replying with flaming darts to fire the wooden platforms, the main attack was launched. It kept up right through the day, the archers on either side trying to pick off their opponents, and the air being filled all the time with the windy cry of missiles. July in Jerusalem is hot. Beneath a brazen sky the men toiled at the ropes on the mangonels while others rolled up stone ammunition, and the dust rose from the walls and beneath the wheels of the towers as they crept forward. It was not until morning on the following day that the tower commanded by Godfrey de Bouillon had finally reached the wall near Herod's Gate. By noon his men had run a bridge across to the top of the battlements. Soon scaling ladders were in place – despite the fire and scalding water and oil that rained down – and the first men were astride the threshold of Jerusalem. Shortly afterwards Robert of Normandy's men, who were on Godfrey's right, also managed to establish themselves on the wall. The Moslems began to retreat, the Damascus Gate was opened, and the Crusaders burst in. The city at once became the scene of fierce hand-to-hand fighting – something at which the Normans, like the Vikings, always excelled.

All afternoon long, in the Year of Our Lord 1099, the men who had taken the Cross – who had professed their adoration of the Prince of Peace – waded through blood in that city 'which He had loved so much that He wished there to save the world'. While Iftikhar-ad-Dowla, together with the remnants of his troops, shut himself up in the citadel, the Crusaders vented their rage and murderous impulses on all whom

The south facade of the Church of the Holy Sepulchre, Jerusalem.

they came across. Fortunately for them, the native Christians had been expelled from the city at the beginning of the siege. There can be little doubt that they too would have fared no better than the other inhabitants when the *furor Normanorum* took over. In the smoke and dust of conquest distinctions of age, caste, or creed passed unrecognised. It was not only the Moslems who were slaughtered in their thousands. The unfortunate Jews – who might have hoped for humane treatment in what was after all *their* city first and foremost – were spared no more than Arabs, Turks or Sudanese. When they took refuge in their main synagogue, despite their protests that they had never aided the Moslems (of which they were accused), it was burned about their ears. The Jewish and the Moslem community perished on that fateful day, leaving Jerusalem – a city where under its former rulers some reasonable religious tolerance had been exercised – almost empty of inhabitants.

Something died with the capture of Jerusalem. It was something incomprehensible (because intangible) to these violent soldiers of the North. It was the possibility of a rational *modus vivendi* being worked out between the Crescent and the Cross. Alexius, that flexible and astute Byzantine Emperor, would have managed things differently. He would have played upon the fears of the governor, stirred up dissidents within the city walls, and would have worked out a solution that gave the city to the Christians, while not denying to Jews and Moslems alike access to the places which were part of their faith as well. The Moslem world would never forget what had happened at Jerusalem. Even though in later years Christian rulers in the East would quite often come to terms of *rapprochement* with their neighbours, what had been done at Jerusalem was something that could never be forgotten. The seeds of the ultimate expulsion of all Christians from the East were sown on that day when the Dome of the Rock (whence Mahomet was said to have ascended to Heaven) was sacked and pillaged, and when men, women and children alike were massacred by the 'Franks' – that generic word for any European, which was to become a term of opprobrium and loathing in the East.

Out of the defenders of the city only Iftikhar-ad-Dowla and his small garrison were spared and allowed to leave – and this only because he had handed over to Raymond of Toulouse a large amount of treasure in return for his safety. Meanwhile the carnage continued. Raymond of Aguilers relates that, when he walked through the streets to the Temple on the following morning, blood and corpses were up to his knees. On the night of the 15th, 'sobbing for excess of joy', the Crusaders entered the Church of the Holy Sepulchre. Their goal was reached. They bowed their heads over their blood-stained hands.

The Seal of the King of Jerusalem, showing the city's three major landmarks : the Dome of the Rock, the Citadel and the Holy Sepulchre.

The Problems of Success

A runner sets himself a target, and reaches it. After that the actualities of life immediately surround the exhausted victor. It is the same with war as with sport. Beyond the immediate aim of capturing a city or a country, something which in itself establishes a simplicity of purpose, there must lie an ultimate aim or ambition. The Crusaders, from the very beginning of their enterprise, had their eyes fixed upon the goal: Jerusalem. It had seemed that once this was achieved, all problems would vanish.

Men are less simple now. Military leaders, whether they like it or not, have usually had established for them by their civil leaders – politicians or, in rare cases, statesmen – a political objective. Beyond the conquered enemy, the ruins of his land and cities, there must lie a purpose of reconstruction, and the redirection of labour and resources. 'Unconditional surrender' is not a political aim. Conquered Jerusalem lay at the feet of the Crusaders who now held, or thought they did, the lands that Jerusalem had commanded. They had cut their way through Turkish Asia, had freed cities for Byzantine control, and had fought successfully through Syria to liberate Jerusalem. Having done so they had little or no idea of what to do next. Should the city be handed over to Alexius or to the Pope, or should it become the capital from which they themselves would administer a kingdom to which all Christians might freely come to worship? Almost inevitably this great treasure (not laid up in heaven but very much on earth) became the bone of dissension between the nobles. Bohemund had secured Antioch for himself, Baldwin Edessa, but the great debate inevitably centred around the ownership of the principate or kingdom that Jerusalem must become. Certainly the Moslems would never let them rest secure in their possession of this city, which was the prize jewel in the crown of three Faiths.

Had Bishop Adhemar lived, there can be no doubt as to the outcome. Pope Urban II had clearly appointed him the leader of the Crusade. The Holy City, captured in a war which had the papal blessing, must surely come under the rule of the Church. Alexius hardly merited consideration now, for he had come neither to Antioch nor to Jerusalem to help them. The claims of the Byzantines might therefore be dismissed, but ecclesiastical claims not so readily. The unfortunate fact was that there was no churchman anywhere approaching the calibre of Adhemar who could command the allegiance and respect of both nobles and commoners. Only Arnulf, Robert's chaplain, was ever seriously considered. A worldly prelate, he had not made himself popular with the rank and file by his disbelief (along with Adhemar) of the truth of Peter Bartholomew's vision of the lance.

The most serious candidates for the position of commander-in-chief or defender of the Holy City were Raymond of Toulouse and Godfrey

Christ leading the Crusaders: from an early fourteenth-century Apocalypse

de Bouillon. Bohemund and Baldwin, as has been seen, had already established their claims to territorial dominion elsewhere – having perhaps been perspicacious enough to see that Jerusalem would always be a golden apple coveted by every Moslem and many Christians. The only other possible candidate was Robert of Normandy but he, unlike so many others, had been sincere in his Crusading vows. Quite apart from the fact that he had his own problems back in Normandy, he had joined the Crusade to liberate the Holy City. Once this was done, and its future administration secured, he and his men would return to Europe.

Raymond was suspect among his colleagues because he had shown only too clearly from the beginning of the Crusade that he regarded himself as its secular leader. Despite his power and wealth, he had not displayed any outstanding qualities of leadership during the numerous actions since the army had first crossed into Asia. His personal bravery could not be discounted, but there was – despite everything – a suspicion of his motives, not least occasioned by the fact that he was known to be a supporter of the Emperor. Godfrey on the other hand was just as brave, wholeheartedly devoted to the aims of the Crusade, and a man of genuine piety. In fact, one of the things which militated against him was that Godfrey was just a little too pious for most of the nobles. As William of

Mahomet the Prophet preaching his last sermon: from A Chronology of Ancient Nations *by Al-Biruni, c.1307.*

89

Tyre records: 'If he was in a church where he had attended Mass or some other service, he would not depart'. While his followers were happy to leave at the conclusion of the service, Godfrey would linger on, eager to hear tales from the lives of the Saints, so that 'by the time they did get away they would find that their meal was cold'. But it was seen in the final analysis, and conclusively demonstrated during the urgent lobbying that went on, that Godfrey de Bouillon was probably the best choice. Despite this, the crown was first of all offered to Raymond. To the surprise of his contemporaries and of subsequent historians, he turned it down. His ostensible reason for doing so, the pious one that he had no wish to reign in the city where Christ had been crucified, must be immediately suspect, knowing his record of ambition and intrigue. The fact almost certainly was that he still had his eye on a principality established at Tripoli, which could be far more prosperous and lucrative without being the burden that Jerusalem must inevitably be.

Godfrey accordingly was chosen. Refusing to accept the crown for the same reason that Raymond had given, he was, by his own wishes, declared not 'King', but 'Advocate of the Holy Sepulchre'. This meant in effect that he was to be its defender but no more. Raymond, despite his refusal (which he had perhaps thought would prevent any other from claiming sovereignty in Jerusalem) was embittered by the choice of Godfrey de Bouillon. He refused to hand over the citadel, which had been surrendered to him personally by Iftikhar-ad-Dowla. He later reliquished it and it ended up, after a series of complicated transactions, in the hands of Godfrey. The latter's first task was to repulse a threatened attack on the city.

The army which had been summoned out of Egypt to come to Jerusalem's relief was now encamped at Ascalon some thirty-five miles east of Jerusalem on the coast. Leaving a small garrison behind, Godfrey marched out from Jerusalem, Raymond and Robert of Normandy accompanying him. The Egyptians had possibly hoped to use their army more as a threat, or a bargaining counter, than anything else. Indeed, if the diplomatic capabilities of Emperor Alexius had been to hand, there seems little doubt that even at this late stage some *rapprochement* could have been made between the Latins and the Moslems. The former, however, understood little except warfare. Heightened by their conquest of Jerusalem, supremely self-confident, the Crusaders carried all before them in a type of battle that exactly suited the armoured

Opposite: *Crusader fleet in the Bosporus : from* Livres des Passages d'Outremer, *fifteenth-century manuscript.*

Affin quil ne seble
que par enuie
ennup ou faulte
dauoir assez veu
listoire doultre mer Je naye de
laisse la conqueste de consta
tinople faicte par les francois
Je la toucheray mais en tres
brief en ces pns passages auf
quelz elle nappartiet directemt

par ce qlle fut faicte par xpi
ens fur xpiens. En la cite de
Jadres assiegiee ou procham
precedent article ariuerét
mahieu de mont morenty
et plusieurs autres seignes
et pelerins francois. Et en
telle mesmes cite virt par
deuers les pelerins Alexe
filz de kirsac Jadis empeur

cavalry. Ascalon was a crushing defeat for the Moslems. The Egyptian army was overwhelmed, its leaders only just managing to save themselves by fleeing to the safety presented by the walls of Ascalon itself.

The citizens now made a grave mistake. Instead of sending a delegation to Godfrey, who was after all 'Advocate' of Jerusalem, they sent one to Raymond, saying that they would surrender to him but to no one else. Godfrey quite naturally refused to agree to this kind of conduct. The hostility between him and Raymond flamed out into the open. The latter, as Sir John Glubb remarks in *The Course of Empire*, '. . . had nearly won Tripoli for himself but Godfrey had compelled him to march on Jerusalem. He had occupied the citadel of Jerusalem, but had been manoeuvred out of it. Now, for the third time, Godfrey was thwarting him.' The most probable reason that the Moslems were prepared to submit to Raymond was that the only survivors from Jerusalem had been those in the tower which Raymond had occupied. They knew well enough the fate that had befallen the rest of the townsfolk and garrison. Not for the first, nor for the last time, was the memory of 15 July to fall like a sword between the aspirations of Moslem and Christian to come to workable terms in the affairs of the East. Raymond in his fury now deserted Godfrey, persuading Robert of Normandy to follow him. The two main supports of the army – both of whom had distinguished themselves in the recent action – marched northward. With the forces left at his disposal Godfrey had no chance of capturing Ascalon. The city remained for years to come like a lance leaning into the side of the Christian territory of Jerusalem.

The First Crusade was to all intents and purposes over after the capture of Jerusalem. That had been the objective, and it had been attained. The future remained obscure and fraught with peril. Some, like Robert of Normandy, left for Europe, feeling that their mission was accomplished. Others, like Raymond and Baldwin and Bohemund, had their own concerns to look after in establishing principalities in the East. By the autumn of 1099 Godfrey de Bouillon was left in charge of Jerusalem with only a few hundred supporters of any consequence, and some 2,000 men. With these, surrounded by Moslem enemies, he was expected to maintain what was in due course to become the Latin Kingdom of Jerusalem. The writing was plain upon the wall – more men from western Europe would be needed to hold this somewhat unenviable fortress-city. Before the departure of Robert of Normandy and Robert

Opposite: *The Coronation of Frederick II, Holy Roman Emperor, as King of Sicily : fifteenth-century manuscript.*

of Flanders Godfrey had a formal meeting with them, and charged them to make known in Europe the necessity for reinforcements if Jerusalem was to be held. He could find no other reliable supporter except Tancred, Bohemund's nephew, whom he appointed Prince of Galilee. For the moment, deriving from their success in Antioch, Jerusalem, and Ascalon, the remnants of the Latin army of occupation might live on their reputation. Inevitably it would not be long before this was in danger from the Moslem sea that surrounded them.

Centre: *Sword, c.1200-50.*
Left: *Sword made for Henry II's grandson, Otto IV, c. 1200.*
Right: *Early thirteenth-century sword.*

Weapons of Victory

It is common enough to talk of the conquests of the Crusaders, the battles in which they fought, the political chaos that largely surrounded them (and sometimes engulfed them), but the means by which they achieved their successes – at least initially – are often forgotten. Turning aside for a moment from Godfrey de Bouillon at Jerusalem with a skeleton force, Tancred as Prince of Galilee, Robert of Normandy and Robert of Flanders *en route* for Europe, Baldwin at Edessa, Bohemund at Antioch, and Raymond of Toulouse temporarily settled with his men at Latakia, it is worth asking the question: What had established these Latins in an area of the world so strange and so distant from their own western Europe? Forgetting, not as irrelevant but as accepted, the religious as well as selfish motives which drove them to their expedition, it is the execution of it that is sometimes overlooked by contemporary chroniclers and later historians. The success of the First Crusade must be seen as stemming largely from one instrument – the sword.

One of the oldest weapons in the art of warfare, the sword which gave Jerusalem to the Crusaders was the direct descendant of the Viking sword that had originated in Scandinavia. It had then triumphed from Finland to northern France, from the Shetlands and the Hebrides to England, Ireland, Germany, and Russia. Even before the Normans, their 'Northmen' ancestors had taken the Viking sword as far afield as Spain, and through the Mediterranean to the Holy Land. 'Viking swords', writes Frederick Wilkinson in *Arms and Armour*, 'were cleverly designed for easy use in action, and this was achieved by tapering the blade towards the point – it meant that there was less weight at the point, so permitting freer movement . . . the style of hilt varied considerably, and as many as nine have been identified. Most have a simple cross-guard, either straight or slightly drooping, and it was in the pommel that there were so many variations.'

95

Such swords were primarily slashing weapons: the mark of nearly all primitive swords before the use of the point had been clearly understood. The Romans with their *gladius* (which could also be used as a slashing sword), tended to concentrate on the use of the point, and it was this that gave them the advantage over so many of their barbarian opponents. The Norman sword was an improved version of the Viking weapon, more elaborate in the pommel, and having a shallow groove, known as the fuller, cut down its length in order to reduce the weight. The fuller is quite often erroneously described as 'the blood gutter'. The hand was protected by a crossguard slightly more elaborate than that found on Viking weapons, with two arms or quillons either straight or curving slightly downwards to arrest the passage of another sword along its length. Such swords were designed for one-handed use, and it is not until later that one finds the sword with a hilt long enough to allow for a two-handed grip. Although primarily a slashing weapon it could nevertheless be used at the point, or 'foining', as this early style of fencing was called. Its usage was best demonstrated when the knights had dismounted from the horses and had formed an iron ring. Coupled with the

Forging armour : a smith fashions a helmet while another checks the trueness of a sword's blade : from an early thirteenth-century manuscript.

weight of the man behind it and its own impetus the Norman sword could cleave through an iron helmet and cut a man down to the shoulders. Graves which have been exhumed in recent years on the sites of old battlefields have revealed the skeletons of men who had been cloven from shoulder down to thigh bone or lost both arms, or in one case both legs, due to what must have been a scything blow aimed at the knees.

The sword was housed in a scabbard, hung normally by leather straps on the left-hand side, although the possibility – as in boxing – of sometimes coming up against a lefthander or 'south-paw' must have remained a challenge. The scabbard was made of wooden strips covered with leather, having a metal guard mounted round the mouth and a metal chape at the tip. Usually the scabbard and its fastening were worn over the soldier's chain mail, although sometimes the sword is depicted with only the hilt projecting from the mail, the latter having been cut so as to allow the sword to ride beneath the mail jerkin.

Hot, cumbersome, but effectively defensive mail leggings and shirt with aventail (to protect the neck and chin).

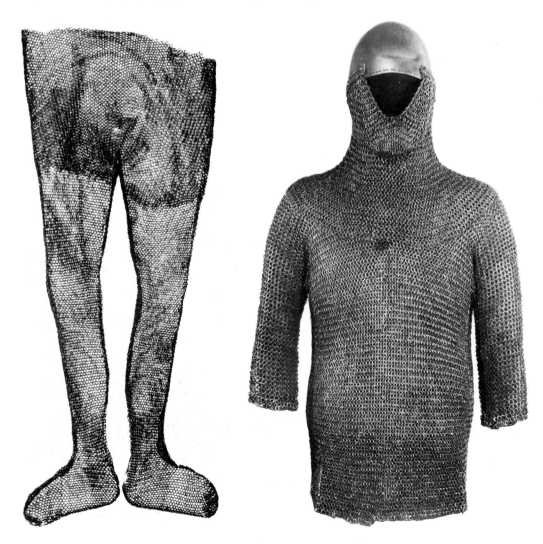

The period of the Crusades was predominantly the Age of Mail. Although the development of plate armour had begun, it was not until the fourteenth and fifteenth centuries that the craft of the armourer had evolved sufficiently to construct angular and fluted metal surfaces which would deflect a sword blow. But, by that time, the sword itself had changed and was primarily used as a thrusting weapon. Plate armour, in fact, had been widely used in the Roman world, but it had almost disappeared subsequent to the barbarian invasions of the western empire. Its only survivors were the shield and the helmet. The former was at this time made more often than not of wood, hardened leather, or leather laid over a wooden surface. The Norman helmet was eminently functional, designed to afford maximum protection, and without any of the elaborate decorative devices of later centuries. Usually of conical shape, it provided deflection for any blow aimed at the head. The nose, face and cheeks were largely protected by the nasal, a bar projecting downwards from the rim to ward off a slashing cut at the face. In some cases there was a similar bar at the back to protect the neck. Most Norman helmets were made with a framework of bronze or iron, and were lined with plates of the same metal. The finest, and far the strongest, were hammered out of a single piece of iron. To protect the wearer's head from the metal and to cushion the shock of any blow the interior was lined with quilted or padded material. Under the midsummer heat of the East, when temperatures are often in the 100's (Fahrenheit), it can hardly have been pleasant to wear. Many of the knights in lieu of the metal helmet wore a *coif*, which was a close-fitting hood made out of chain mail.

Mail would seem to have originated in the East, although the *byrnie*, a shirt of mail, is often referred to in Icelandic sagas. A useful form of body defence, it was, initially at any rate, not only difficult but expensive to make – so that the wearers were usually wealthy. Knights, for instance, would wear mail, while foot soldiers and others had to content themselves with jackets of leather or quilted material. First of all the metal had to be drawn out into wire. After this it was wrapped around a former and cut into open-ended circlets. The links were then interwoven, the open ends being flattened and drilled and riveted together. Constructed of these circular rings it was usually made in four- or five-fold lengths. It was shaped to the body and 'built' in much the same manner as a jersey of wool. Flexible, and sufficiently supple to allow easy freedom of movement, mail would ward off glancing arrows or sword cuts. Often the sleeves only came down to the elbow, but the tendency was to extend them right down to the wrist with, as a sophisticated development,

Soldiers wearing Norman helmets defend their castle by hurling rocks at attackers: from the Bury Bible, *c.1121.*

mittens of mail that covered the back of the hands. The short jacket or *haubergon* came down no farther than the waist, but the long overcoat-length *hauberk* reached to the knees and was quite often accompanied by leggings of chain mail. Separate 'stockings' covering the exposed front of the legs were also used, being laced up with leather thongs at the back. Clearly no skin, however hardened, could tolerate such a garment next to it, and beneath his coat of mail the armoured man wore a padded or quilted jacket. Designed primarily for use in the cold weather of the North, it is astonishing how the Crusaders managed to endure this combination in Asia and the Levant. As Charles Ffoulkes commented in *The Armourer and his Craft*: 'It is one of the mysteries in the history of armour how the Crusaders can have fought under the scorching sun of the East in thick quilted garments covered with excessively heavy chain mail, for this equipment was so cumbersome to take on and off that it must frequently have been worn night and day . . .'

Quite apart from this, mail had other disadvantages such as the danger of links splitting under a blow and perforating the skin. The weight pressed mainly on the shoulders and, because of this and the weight of the padding, it was hardly possible to take more than a wide swinging blow at one's opponent. An additional disadvantage was that, as the sword-arm rose, so the mail tended to collect in folds at the elbow. The action of raising the arm inevitably dragged upward the folds of mail beneath armpit and waist. Nevertheless, as the constant use of mail throughout these centuries proves, it was more than useful in a protective sense. Whether the wearers were formed into a defensive circle against mounted attackers, or standing guard on castle walls, mail would deflect most arrow strokes and gave a considerable advantage in hand-to-hand combat.

The Moslem enemy tended to rely more on mobility and on the use of mounted archers than did the Latin invaders of their lands. The crescent-shaped Arabic and Asiatic scimitar was an excellent cutting weapon, particularly when used by a mounted warrior since it was lighter and enjoyed more flexibility in use than the Norman sword. When it came to hand-to-hand combat, however, at which the Normans like the Vikings excelled, the greater weight of the northern sword gave it an advantage. The famous sword-blades of Damascus and of Khurasan had been long established, and the cutting-power of a well-made scimitar with its highly acute-angled section was very considerable. The Moslems, even the wealthy, did not value armour as highly as the Christians, although chain mail was not uncommon among them. Relying, however, on dashing cavalry attacks, eschewing as far as possible close-range work, their loose clothes gave them a considerable advantage in their climate. The archer, the bowman, mounted more often than not, was the enemy whom the Europeans would learn to fear over the long decades in the East.

The bow is one of the oldest weapons known in history and, except for Australia, has been found in recorded evidence since the early Stone Age. In Asia and the Near East the bow had long been the dominant weapon, and both Turk and Arab made extensive use of it in warfare as well as in hunting. The wooden bow used in Europe usually weighed between 30 and 50 lb dependent on its thickness, the 'weight' of the bow being measured by the number of pounds required for the archer to draw an arrow to its head. The arrow was usually about 28 in, and the bow about 5 ft long. The eastern bow was different, dating back certainly to as early as the Assyrians (and possibly having its origins in the Far East). Shorter than the European bow and, for obvious reasons, having evolved without the advantage of suitable woods like yew, the bow as used by the Moslems during these centuries was composite made, being of horn, wood, and sinew, in that order from front to back. Short and very strong, weighing up to 100 lb, the eastern bow was so resilient that, when unstrung, it had such reflexion or recurvation that it could be bent forward. This reflexed shape meant that the bow, when strung, was in such a high degree of stress – even before the arrow was drawn – that its casting power or quickness in action was far greater than the wooden bow's. It was not until the full development of the 6-ft long-bow, 'the only projectile weapon of Great Britain' as it has been called, that the Scythian/Parthian/Eastern bow was eclipsed. But this was not until the fifteenth century, when the English long-bowman would finally proclaim the end of the mounted knight in armour. During their many campaigns in the East the Latins used European bowmen as well as native mercenaries. The long-bow would of course have been useless to a mounted rider, but the short bow had given the Turks and the Arabs most of the lands which the Christians now disputed with them.

Other weapons that the northern invaders brought with them, or evolved to a higher degree than the ancient hand-weapons of the East, were those generally known as pole-arms or staff weapons. Largely descended from agricultural implements like the scythe or billhook,

Mounted Saracen archers, of the army of Caliph al-Mahdi, besiege a city: from an early fourteenth century manuscript.

Many of the weapons used in the twelfth to fourteenth centuries.

From the Maciejowski Bible, *early thirteenth-century.*

they included long spiked clubs, the pole-axe, and the halberd (a long-handled axe with two spikes, one at the top and the other at the rear of the axe-head). The bill was another pole weapon having a cutting edge ending in a hook. Flails, studded iron balls on the end of a short length of chain attached to a short sturdy haft, and the mace, a heavy iron head on a reinforced wooden shaft, were for close combat work. The mace was sometimes called the 'morning star' after the German name for it. There were many variants on these basic types, including the war hammer which had a stout pick-point for piercing armour, and the glaive which had a long spear-shape, one side of which was broadened into a cutting edge. Both Christians and Moslems used spears for casting, and for holding a defensive position against cavalry.

The Europeans, as is clear, were better armoured and, all in all, better weaponed than the Moslem enemy. Nevertheless the Moslems had fine horses, fine archers, and were – at least in these early years – far more familiar with the terrain than their opponents. The horses used by the knights were not, as is sometimes supposed, heavy and ponderous like cart-horses. Chain mail was not all that heavy and, even after plate-armour came in, a full suit of it might weigh little more than 60 lb. (Tests conducted at the New York Metropolitan Museum have shown that a plate-armoured man can run, jump, and even leap into the saddle without much difficulty.) The really heavy horse, the *destrier* or Great Horse, was never used on campaigns but only for the joust. Much lighter and faster was the courser, used for battle and looking rather like a modern show-jumper or heavy hunter. But in all the individual battles and hard-fought campaigns that were to follow the establishment of Latin colonies, principalities, or kingdoms in the East, it was the sword which largely decided the outcome. On some occasions, such as the famous battle at the Horns of Hattin in the twelfth century when a Crusader army was overwhelmed, this was almost entirely due to mistaken strategy and plain stupidity. As they had shown at Ascalon and elsewhere, the Normans and their followers were superior to their enemies so long as they chose a ground where the weight of their armoured charge could be fully deployed or where, fighting man-to-man, their mail and their three-foot swords were more than a match for their enemies.

The Kingdom

On Christmas Day, 1100, Godfrey's brother Baldwin was crowned king in Jerusalem. Godfrey had died in the summer of that year. Despite attempts by the then patriarch of Jerusalem, Dagobert, to ensure the election of his own patron, Bohemund, there was too much opposition to the latter. He had, in any case, previously declined the honour. Largely on the strength of the good reputation that Godfrey had won, his dying wish that his brother should succeed him prevailed. During his short period of administering Jerusalem, Godfrey had proved himself an excellent and conscientious ruler; brave in battle but not so hidebound in his views that he was incapable of seeing the necessity of establishing friendly relationships, where possible, with local Arab rulers. It was hoped that Baldwin would emulate him and that, by forestalling both Bohemund and papal aspirations for the rulership of the city, a permanent kingdom might be founded which would neither be subject to pressures from Normandy nor from Rome. Dagobert, who crowned Baldwin King of Jerusalem, was in effect (and much against his will) giving his sanction to the construction of a secular kingdom. The idea of a theocracy, which Pope Urban II had always dreamed of, was thus finally destroyed.

The establishment of this Kingdom of Jerusalem was not only a blow to the Church but to the Normans of Antioch. If Bohemund had not himself been captured in a battle with the Turks shortly after the death of Godfrey it is very probable that Jerusalem would have been his. Baldwin's task was not an easy one. Although a number of knights and others had elected to settle in the country it would seem that he had little more than 300 knights for the defence not only of Jerusalem, but of Haifa, Jaffa, and Ramlah. This was clearly impossible if he were to be faced with any real organised opposition. He swiftly made every attempt to enlist the aid of all those who would enable him to retain his hold on a house which did indeed seem to be built upon sand. The fact that the Latin Kingdom of Jerusalem survived at all can largely be traced to its first king. Baldwin possessed the physical and mental abilities to impress his contemporaries, whether fellow-Christians or Moslems. Tall and goodlooking, he had the bearing of a king, while his early clerical training served him in good stead as an administrator. Cynical in politics, where Godfrey had been somewhat ingenuous, Baldwin was also as able a diplomat as any of his time. It was diplomacy

The crowning of Baldwin I, as King of Jerusalem, from William Tyres History, *c. 1280.*

as well as, or even more than, the sword that was to be needed in the complicated affairs of this new kingdom.

Temporary assistance must be sought at any and every level. Baldwin had no scruples. The ships of Genoa, ever eager to expand their trading interests in the East, were consistently used to further the safety of the kingdom. In 1101 the Genoese assisted Baldwin at Caesarea, in the following year at Tartous, than at Acre and Jubail in 1104, and five years later at Tripoli. There was no Crusading zeal about the Genoese. As far as they were concerned the whole thing was a commercial trans-action. They lent the ships, the men, and their skilled siege-engineers, in return for which they obtained trading concessions in the ports that now came under Baldwin's rule. Their agreement, congenial also to Baldwin, was that in every captured city they should have one third of the plunder – a temporary enrichment which served to make good any losses as well as to pay for the expedition – while, as a long-term invest-ment, they had their trading-quarter in the town concerned. Aware as was everyone of the great rivalry between Genoa and Venice, Baldwin was equally happy to make use of the Venetians on similar terms. Thus, against Beirut and Sidon in 1110, it was the Venetians who provided the ships and technical knowledge for the assault of these important cities. In view of the ancestry of so many of the nobles who had cap-tained the First Crusade, and who were now struggling to establish themselves in the East, it is worth noting that prominent in the capture of Sidon was a Viking king, Sigurd of Norway.

All this activity would not in the long run have availed the Latin Kingdom of Jerusalem had the latter not possessed an intangible quality, something which no other city in the East could boast. As Sir Ernest Barker put it: 'Jerusalem, like Rome, had the shadow of a mighty name to lend prestige to its ruler; and as residence in Rome was one great reason of the strength of the medieval papacy, so was residence in Jerusalem a reason for the ultimate supremacy of the Lotharingian kings. Jerusalem attracted the flow of pilgrims from the West as Antioch never could; and though the great majority of the pilgrims were only birds of passage, there were always many who stayed in the East.'

This steady flow of new immigrants was a large source of Jerusalem's strength. Antioch, although it lay in one of the most fertile areas of the East, suffered from having strong Moslem powers in its neighbourhood and from being near to any sources of invasion from the north. Further-more Alexius, who on the surface of it at least seemed to have resigned himself to the loss of Jerusalem, continued to claim Antioch as a former Byzantine city and one which should be returned to him. He managed to manipulate the intense rivalry that existed between Raymond of Toulouse and Bohemund. The former not only allied himself with Alexius but, by doing so, managed to establish the principality of Tripoli which barred the expansion of Antioch to the south, while the army of Alexius prevented any encroachment to the north. Bohemund, was perhaps the outstanding figure of his time, but he failed because of an ambition that outran his assets. Unwise enough to attack the Eastern empire in 1108, he was ignominiously defeated. He died in obscurity in Apulia three years later.

Baldwin, on the other hand, had extended his small kingdom as far south as Aila (modern Aqaba) on the Gulf of Aqaba by the time of his death in 1118. He had planted a castle at Showbek to the north of this, and had even projected an invasion of Egypt. It was during the course of this that, having reached as far as the Pelusiac branch of the Nile, he fell mortally ill. He left a kingdom that stretched from Beirut to Al-Arish, almost on the borders of Egypt, but which, constrained by Jordan to the east and the kingdom of Damascus to the south, had little breadth. Its geographical boundaries and its situation in political terms were not so dissimilar from those of Israel in the second half of the twentieth century. Like Israel it was surrounded by Arabic enemies, its religious beliefs were different, and its principal backing came from abroad. The fact that it managed to exist at all was primarily due to superior weaponry and tactics, and to the dissensions which prevailed amongst the Moslems and prevented them from uniting in one determined assault to throw their opponents into the sea.

When Baldwin had become ruler of Jerusalem his nephew, who became Baldwin II (Baldwin I died childless), had been left by his uncle in charge of Edessa. Married to an Armenian wife, Baldwin II was an experienced soldier and a wily, indeed unscrupulous, politician. In the web of power, politics and intrigue that surrounded him, he had need to be. The rich area around Tripoli had now come within the influence of the Kingdom of Jerusalem and, in 1130, Baldwin II became the governor of Antioch. All the harbours of Palestine and Syria, with the exception only of Ascalon, had fallen to the Crusaders during a series of battles and campaigns lasting over quarter of a century. None of this would have been possible if the Moslem powers that surrounded the Latin kingdom had not been divided in interminable strife.

The effect of these new Latin lands and estates upon Europe, and of the Kingdom of Jerusalem itself, was profound. What had begun as a religious dream, later fuelled by personal ambitions, was gradually transformed during the twelfth century into a very concrete fact. A colonial problem – something quite new to the thinking of western Europeans – now confronted them. *Outremer* was far from just an extension of Europe, an expansion into some unknown land where the settlers had to cope with unfamiliar problems. All that was to come later, from the time of the Columbian voyages onwards. The fact was that, in the East, the Normans and their followers met with a culture that was quite different to their own, a culture not only alien but superior.

It was hardly surprising that the Europeans, who never at any time numbered more than a few thousands, were deeply influenced by their neighbours and their surroundings. They found, as the Byzantines had done long before them, that to live and trade in the East they had themselves to become somewhat orientalised. The Crusaders and pilgrims of earlier days had been disgusted to find that the Byzantines

Pilgrims: detail from a fresco by Andrea da Firenze in the Spanish chapel of S Maria Novella, Florence, c.1365.

permitted an area of their 'God-defended City' to be set aside as a Moslem quarter and even, unthinkable blasphemy, a mosque to be erected for the infidels' worship. But they themselves now lived surrounded by mosques, in a sea of people who believed in one God certainly, but not in a divine intercessor, Jesus Christ. They found in their dealings with Moslems – and inevitably they had to make many a judicious treaty in order to survive – that by and large the latter were well-mannered. They were no more untrustworthy in business matters than Christians (and sometimes less so), and the pattern of their lives was more subtle and sophisticated than that which obtained in most of Europe. In the process of daily contact, and of political as well as military give-and-take, the conquerors were to some extent the conquered. 'Captive Greece', the Roman poet Horace had written twelve centuries before, 'made captive her rude conqueror'. He was referring to the effect that Greek art, science, literature, manners, and morals had had upon the Romans. The same could certainly be said of the effect of the Levant upon the Latins. Norman barons and clerics, merchants, men-at-arms, and peasants, found that they were not so much the donors of a culture as the recipients.

In one respect the agricultural methods and farming techniques of the Latins showed them as the superiors of the previous inhabitants. The feudal system of Europe was imported into an exotically unfamiliar environment and seems to have thriven. Although many of the Moslems had emigrated after the Crusaders' invasions, those who remained, as well as the Latin peasant-farmers, paid a percentage of their earnings to their local lord. That they were not unhappy and that the system worked better than that in Moslem-dominated areas is evidenced by the chronicle of Ibn Jubayr, who made a pilgrimage from Granada to Mecca in 1183, returning via Damascus and Acre. In his travels he had ample opportunity to observe the conditions in the occupied lands:

'We moved from Tibnin – may God destroy it – at daybreak on Monday. Our way lay through continuous farms and ordered settlements whose inhabitants were all Muslims, living comfortably with the Franks. God protect us from such temptation! They surrender half their crops to the Franks at harvest-time, and pay as well a poll-tax of one dinar and five qirat for each person. Other than that, they are not interfered with, save for a light tax on the fruits of trees. Their houses and all their effects are left to their full possession. All the coastal cities occupied by Franks are managed in this fashion, their rural districts, the villages and farms, belonging to the Muslims. But their hearts have been seduced, for they observe how unlike them in ease and comfort are their brethren in the

Muslim regions under their [Muslim] governors. This is one of the misfortunes afflicting the Muslims. The Muslim community bewails the injustice of a landlord of its own faith, and applauds the conduct of its opponent and enemy, the Frankish landlord, and is accustomed to justice from him . . . The Christians impose a tax on the Muslims in their land which gives them full security; and likewise the Christian merchants pay a tax upon their goods in Muslim lands. Agreement exists between them and there is equal treatment in all cases. The soldiers engage themselves in their war, while the people are at peace and the world goes to him who conquers.' (Translated by R J C Broadbent).

In any dealings with their overlord the villagers approached the headman or *Rais* with their problems and complaints. He himself dealt with the *drogmannus* (dragoman). The latter was usually a Latin, who acted as secretary and accountant for his lord, and naturally an Arabicspeaker. It was hardly surprising that, as the years went by and generations of Europeans grew up in Syria and Palestine, they became markedly different in manners and attitudes from their forebears, and especially from the newcomers who streamed annually to *Outremer*, some bent on the salvation of their souls, and others on fighting the 'pagan' or acquiring land for themselves. The 'old Near East hands', if such one may term them, had long found that in order to survive they often had to conclude treaties with Turks, with Arabs, and with Egyptians. Familiar from daily contact with Moslems, they were familiar also with Greeks who were members of the Orthodox Greek Church (regarded as schismatical by Rome), and with Jews. In the somewhat parochial European communities where they had originated it had been easy to believe that there was only one version of Truth. In the East it seemed that many beliefs could live together without undue offence being given. The Moslems, for instance, during their occupation of Jerusalem had tolerated not only a large Jewish community but also a Christian one, and had been prepared to allow the Christians visiting the land to have access to the places which they deemed holy. After all, they were holy to the Moslem too. P H Hitti, translating Usamah ibn Muniqdh, in *An Arab-Syrian Gentleman and Warrior*, shows how a Moslem might well honour Jesus, while still maintaining his reservations. 'I saw one of the Franks come up to al-Amir Mu'in al-Din (may Allah's mercy rest upon his soul) when he was in the Dome of the Rock and say to him "Dost thou want to see God as a child?" Mu'in al-Din said "Yes". The Frank walked ahead of us until he showed us the picture of Mary with Christ (may peace be upon him) as an infant in her lap. He then said, "This is

God as a child". But Allah is exalted far above what the infidels say about him.'

Usamah, it is clear, cannot help despising the Christians for their simplicity and ignorance, although he admits their courage and prowess at fighting – 'the virtues of animals'. He remarks how some of them had taken up eastern ways. He mentions one knight, living at Antioch, whose kitchen was 'clean', who employed Egyptian cooks, and who would eat no pork. He comments also on the difference that existed between those who had lived a long time in the East and the new arrivals, the latter thirsting for blood and despising their compatriots for the many accommodations they had reached with the society that surrounded them.

The fact was that, in the contacts between East and West which resulted from the Crusades, it was Europe that was largely the beneficiary. What Norman lord in the draughty discomfort of his castle in England or France would not gladly have exchanged it for the comforts of a castle, let alone a private dwelling, in the Levant? Elegance and splendour replaced the crude furniture and primitive feeding-habits of the North. The East had long been famed for its sophistication and luxury, eastern cuisine was a far call from the gross simplicity of the Norman board. In a number of the cities there were piped water supplies (for the East had never forgotten Rome) and efficient sewage systems – something quite unknown in Europe for centuries to come. To make sure that drought did not occur during the long hot summers, vast underground cisterns ensured that there was always a plentiful supply of good drinkable water. The interiors of the houses, hung with damask, enriched with fine carpets, with feather beds and elegant furniture, would – and did – amaze the northern visitor. Rather like the Crusaders, when they had first visited Byzantium, he felt himself ill at ease amid such refinements. He disguised his feeling of inferiority by maintaining that such surroundings did not breed real men.

In *Outremer*, where the Byzantines had built their houses and cities upon the traditions of Greece and Rome, and where the Moslems had emulated them (while at the same time importing their own refinements), life was seen as something which under the warm sky of those lands could be lived with comfort and distinction. It was from the East that cushions, stuffed pillows, tapestries, and silks reached northern Europe. It was from the East that beautiful Syrian faience, Egyptian glassware (some so delicate that it was believed in countries like England to be the work of fairies), and even articles of porcelain deriving from the Arabic trade across the Indian Ocean, came to delight and astound the rain- and mist-bound Northerner.

The dress of men was radically changed by the demands of climate and, though the knights still wore their chain-mail into battle, they wore over it a white surcoat made of linen. Over their mail or iron helmets they wore the Arabic kerchief or keffiyeh. In their homes the settlers wisely adopted the burnous and the turban. Their ladies also wore the clothing of the East – so much lighter and more elegant than the heavy wools and velvets of Europe. Long silk dresses were set off by short tunics, heavily embroidered, while in their hair and on their wrists and fingers sparkled delicate enamels, colourful gemstones, and pearls from the Red Sea. Some of the cities even had public baths, a Roman inheritance, while baths were quite commonplace in the private houses of merchants and nobles. Incense from Egypt and perfumes of Syria hung on the air. All this was a far call from austerity and asceticism.

Armed knight and armour-bearer, c.1250.

Failure in the East

The Crusades were above all a continuous process. Hardly a year passed without the arrival of new troops in the Holy Land, sometimes in their hundreds, and more rarely in their thousands. The principal Crusades, those which have been marked as it were with a number, were almost without exception – and that exception being the First – either complete disasters or failures redeemed only by some unlooked for success. (Such was the Fourth Crusade.) The Second has achieved prominence because at its head was Louis VII of France, and in his company was Conrad III of Germany. St Bernard, although somewhat suspicious of Crusading motives, was prevailed upon by Pope Eugenius III (1145-53) to preach the Crusade and it was only owing to his eloquence that Conrad was induced to take the cross. On the surface of it, led by kings, and destined for an area in which there were already friends, fortified cities, castles, and Jerusalem itself, all eager to receive their help, the Second Crusade should have been a success.

The situation that had called it into being was in itself quite grave enough. Edessa, that bulwark of Frankish Syria, had fallen to the *atabeg* (regent) Zengi, who had been the ruler of Mosul since 1127, and who was above all others the arch-enemy of the Latin kingdoms. The years between 1143 – when both the Byzantine Emperor John Comnenus died, and Fulk, King of Jerusalem was killed in a hunting accident – and 1145, when Edessa was securely held against the Latins by Nur-ed-Din, son of Zengi, marked a watershed in the history of the Latin kingdoms of the East. John Comnenus had been one of the greatest Byzantine rulers. He had done more than any other to restore and maintain Byzantine rule in the East, while Fulk had managed during the twelve

Opposite: *John II Commenus, Emperor of the East 1118-43: detail from a mosaic in Santa Sophia.*

years of his reign to cope more than adequately with Zengi's invasions in the north. He had also brilliantly averted Zengi's threat to Damascus by concluding a treaty with the city. In the extraordinarily shifting complexity of eastern affairs the Latins had learned, in the hard school of Levantine power-politics, how to hold their own.

The sudden deaths of these two men, leaving a new emperor, Manuel Comnenus, in Constantinople and a child of twelve years, Baldwin III, as King of Jerusalem (with his mother Melisande as regent), were distinctly unfortunate. With the fall of Edessa on Christmas day 1144, the situation looked desperate for the Christians, while the extinction of this Latin state gave hope to the Moslems. It was in response to this threat to the whole of *Outremer* that the Second Crusade was preached, and that Louis VII pledged himself to bring the soldiers of the West once more to the relief of their brethren in the East.

It is easy, with the benefit of hindsight, to see that the Crusade was doomed from the start. In 1147, when the leaders met to draw up their final plans for the whole operation, two main differences of opinion led to a split from top to bottom in the command. First of all, Manuel Comnenus insisted that all conquests should be in his name, and that the Crusaders should acknowledge this. It was no more than Alexius had asked in 1096, but circumstances had greatly changed. The second question – and one which divided the participants even more – was which route should the Crusading army take. Was it to be by land or by sea? Manuel was eager for the army to proceed by the overland route via Hungary. Thus, coming under the walls of Constantinople, it would become dependent upon Byzantine transport. It would also help to establish the security of his territories during the march south. Conrad, who was related by marriage to Manuel, agreed on the overland route, as did Louis VII. The principal objector to it was Roger of Sicily. The son of Roger I, who had conquered the island – and whose tolerance towards both Arabs and Greeks had produced a Sicilian 'Renaissance' long in advance of that more famous one which has become generally considered the starting-point of modern European history – Roger I had long aimed at the uniting of all Norman conquests in Italy together with his island-kingdom. The Pope had formally invested him 'King of Sicily, Duke of Apulia and Prince of Capua'. (This was very largely as a

Opposite: *A furious battle shows the terrible slaughter of the Crusading wars: from the* Maciejowski Bible, *early thirteenth-century.*

Overleaf: *The Assassin Castle of Masyaf in Syria, the headquarters of Rashid ad-Din Sinan, the 'Old Man of the Mountains'.*

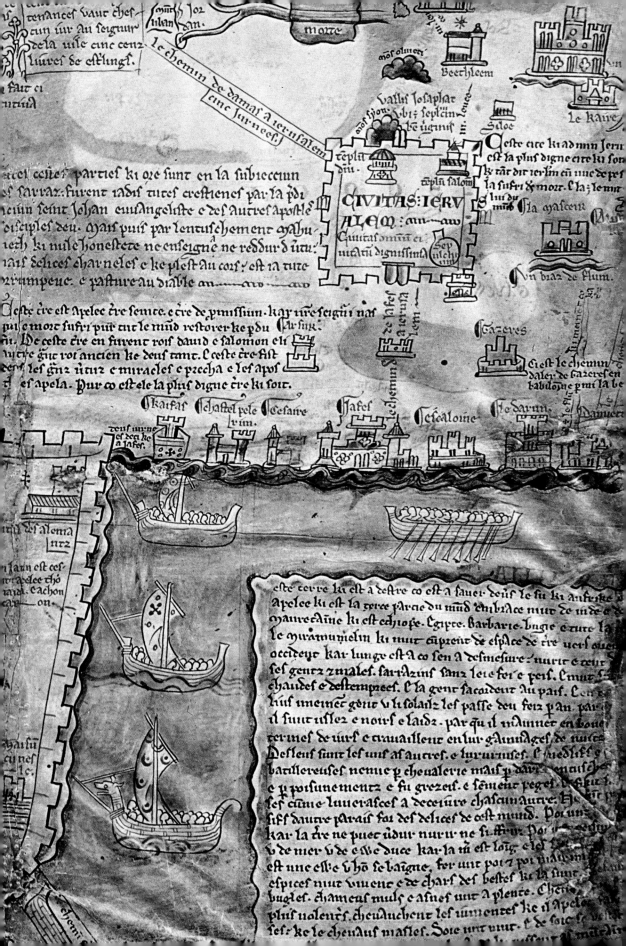

result of having himself been decisively defeated by Roger when he had attempted to invade southern Italy.) One of the greatest kings of Europe, the ruler of Sicily which had become once again – as it had been in Greek days – the principal maritime power in the Mediterranean, Roger was most unwilling to see the Crusaders diverted overland for the convenience of the Byzantines. He had hopes that Crusading fleet, which would necessarily visit Sicily if it came principally from Genoa, might be diverted to the conquest of Constantinople. He saw Greece and possibly all the Byzantine Empire within his grasp. Such hopes were not to be fulfilled for nearly a hundred years when Doge Dandolo of Venice was to achieve Roger's dream. Roger, however, during a reign that lasted until 1154, apart from attacking the Byzantine Empire and challenging the might of Constantinople, and sending an army as far abroad as Thebes – which it sacked and looted – was unable to divert the main course of the Second Crusade.

There was practically no unity among the Crusaders, quite apart from this major divergence between two of the main personalities involved. The northern Germans, indeed, never even made their way across Europe. They turned aside to attack the Wends who lived east of the Elbe river, thus setting in train a war of conquest and an atmosphere of hatred between northern and southern Germany which was to last for a very long time. The English, and the Crusaders from the Low Countries, somewhat naturally elected to take the sea route to the Holy Land. This was an objective which they were late in reaching since they also turned aside: in their case to help Alphonso I of Portugal to capture Lisbon from the Moslems. This was an achievement which, though it had little or nothing to do with their prime objective, certainly helped to reduce Moslem power in Europe, as well as the threat to European ships on the Biscay trade routes. These Crusaders from the North were later to reach the Holy Land where they took part in the successful siege of Damascus. Although this diversion seemed at the time to be irrelevant to the Second Crusade, it was in fact one of the few real achievements of the expedition. It is worth remarking that in subsequent Crusades, such as the Third and Fifth, the English, the Flemings, and the Scandinavians regularly took the sea-route via the Atlantic, and just as regularly helped the native inhabitants of the Iberian peninsula against the Moslem enemy. Britain's long friendship with Portugal – 'the oldest alliance' – stems, in principle at least, from this period.

Opposite: *A page from Matthew Paris's itinerary from London to Jerusalem: drawn in c.1259.*

The overland route, involving passing through Asia Minor as the armies of the First Crusade had done, proved disastrous to Conrad III and the Germans. These Crusaders appear to have heard or learned nothing from the previous experiences of men who had fought against the Turks. They set out from Nicaea in October 1147 with insufficient food-supplies for the long march south and, heavily attacked by the Seljuk army near Dorylaeum, ignored the basic principles of warfare as conducted by armoured men against well-mounted unarmoured troops. Time and again they charged the Turks in classic medieval manner, only to be killed in their hundreds by the elusive bowmen, who naturally would not stand and fight but relentlessly poured their arrows into the dense throng of men. Conrad's army was to all intents and purposes wiped out. The German's feelings of mortification can be easily understood when, having escaped back to Nicaea, he found the army of Louis VII already assembled there and preparing for their own venture into Asia. At any rate the French learned something from the German débâcle. This was, not to venture into the hostile hinterland but to keep to the coast, where a chain of Byzantine castles afforded protection. Even so, they fared very little better than their predecessors. Failing to take account of the winter weather, or failing to establish a winter headquarters and wait for the spring, they marched on via Ephesus, crossed the Maeander river, to reach the inhospitable mountain ranges of Attalia in February 1148. From their Maeander passage onwards, although they were within territory that theoretically was under the control of the Emperor, they suffered nothing but continual attacks by the Seljuk horsemen. At Attalia itself the king and his knights took ship for St Simeon, the port of Antioch. The bulk of the infantry carried on by the coast route through Cilicia to Antioch. Many of them died from cold and starvation on the way, while others were cut down by the enemy. Little more than a handful succeeded in making their way through to Antioch by the spring. The lack of cooperation between Conrad and Louis was largely occasioned by the fact that both were aware that their troops disliked each other almost as much as they did the enemy. Their failure to adopt tactics which had been proved sound in the First Crusade and subsequently over many years in the Holy Land was unforgivable. The leaders of the expedition proved that Europeans had learned little or nothing from the experience of their predecessors in Asia and the Levant.

Conrad, who had wintered in Constantinople with the remains of his force, sailed for Palestine in the spring. On 24 June, 1148, reinforced by fresh troops from France under the banner of the Count of Toulouse – the son of Raymond who had played so large a part in the First Crusade –

Christ crowning Roger II of Sicily : from a twelfth-century mosaic.

the assembled Crusaders and their leaders, Conrad, Louis, and Baldwin III of Jerusalem, met to discuss the recovery of Edessa. An almost unbelievable peak of folly was reached when they decided to turn their combined forces against Damascus. There can be little doubt that the newcomers were largely responsible for this outrageous blunder.

Damascus to them was merely another city inhabited by infidels (dominating, moreover, extremely rich land which could be usefully divided amongst the victors), while its name was a byword for luxury and wealth. Let Edessa wait was their tragic conclusion.

Damascus was the only Moslem state which had successfully resisted Nur-ed-Din, the Latins' greatest enemy. It was also an ally of the Latins. Nur-ed-Din, when he heard the news that the Frankish army had marched against Damascus, must have been almost unable to believe his good fortune. Anar, the vizier of Damascus, after some inconclusive dealings with Nur-ed-Din, turned to the Christians. He still retained friends among the 'old hands', and he had little difficulty in convincing them that, if he and Nur-ed-Din were to conclude an alliance, Moslem unity would be achieved at the expense of all the Latins who lived in the East.

The siege of Damascus, which lasted only five days, was both a farce and a disaster. The Crusaders from Europe were disgusted with the

Damascus: from Matthew Paris's Historia Major II, *c.1240.*

behaviour of their compatriots, whom they saw were in close and friendly contact with Anar and other Moslems, while the Latins from the eastern states regarded the impetuous and ill-advised actions of their 'saviours' with contempt. With their failure before the walls of Damascus the Second Crusade collapsed in ruins. Conrad sailed for Constantinople, where he concluded a treaty with Manuel Comnenus against Roger of Sicily. Louis VII, after spending nearly a year in Palestine, finally sailed for home via Italy where he, for his part, signed a treaty with Roger II against both Conrad and Manuel.

The Crusade which was to have united Latin and German Europe, cemented relations between the Byzantines and the West, restored the kingdom of Edessa, and helped to preserve the Christian kingdoms in the East, fell apart like a patchwork garment. Personal rivalries, national ambitions, and a total lack of understanding between the newcomers and the Latin inhabitants of the Holy Land, all contributed to political, military, and financial ruin. Only Anar, the wily and intelligent vizier of Damascus, emerged with credit and with enhanced security. Even Nur-ed-Din had achieved little or nothing in his campaign against the Frankish kingdoms, except a breathing space to give him strength for the future.

The long-term result of the Second Crusade was the withering of the Crusading spirit in Europe. Totally dispirited by their encounters with the Seljuk Turks (far from a spent force as perhaps they had unwisely imagined), they were disillusioned beyond all measure with the behaviour of the Latins of the Levant. Chafing with personal enmities and smouldering with national rivalries, the Europeans withdrew. If the Crusade of the Princes in 1097 had achieved what the Crusade of the People had failed to do, the Crusade of the Kings was an unmitigated failure. Far from western Christendom being united against the Moslem, and eager to bring help to the Europeans in the Holy Land, it was divided into mutually hostile camps, suspicious of the Byzantines and contemptuous of the defenders of *Outremer*.

Tomb of a Crusader in Dorchester Abbey Church, Oxfordshire.

The Military Orders

One of the most striking features of the Crusades, one of the most unusual events in history indeed, was the emergence after the capture of Jerusalem and the establishment of the Latin Kingdom, of small groups of men trained in the art of war, and dedicated to the preservation of the pilgrim routes and eternal warfare against the Moslem. These were the members of the nobility who formed themselves into associations that came to be known as the Military Orders. 'The Kingdom of Jerusalem', as Richard Barber writes in *The Knight and Chivalry*, 'had arisen in the absence of any planned alternative . . . it was chiefly concerned with preserving its own existence, rather than with the function of guardian of the Holy Places with which it found itself endowed. Yet pilgrims could not be turned away; they had therefore to be protected. In the absence of official action, it was left to a small group of knights to act.'

Founded with the intention of preserving the pilgrims' lives and of serving, as it were, as military police on the troubled roads of Palestine, the first of these groups was granted by King Baldwin in 1118 a place of residence near the Temple in Jerusalem. Taking the same vows as monks – poverty, chastity, and obedience – the Templars, as they came to be known, were ultimately to become one of the richest organisations not only in the East but throughout Europe.

These 'poor knights of Christ', as they called themselves, obtained in due course from Rome the precepts, based largely on the Cistercian rule, by which the conduct of their life was defined. At their head was the Grand Master, enjoying wide powers but constricted none the less by the officers of the Grand Chapter. One of the gravest disadvantages attendant upon the Order, at any rate as far as the Kings of Jerusalem were concerned, was that their only suzerain was the Pope. They con-

Opposite: *Templars ride to battle: from a twelfth-century mural.*

stituted, therefore, a kingdom within a kingdom and, though they would fight against the Moslems, they would not necessarily fight when and where the King wanted them.

Their Grand Master sat in the High Court of the Kingdom, as well as in those of Tripoli and Antioch, but they always put the interests of their Order first and foremost. The Order was soon flourishing throughout Latin Christendom, and every new establishment received rich endowments. Louis VII, for instance, gave them land outside Paris, which became the Order's headquarters in Europe, while Kings of England granted them lands, and Popes allowed them to have their own churches. They drew their members from the nobility but, at any rate to begin with, these were not always the best examples of the ruling class. Bernard de Clairvaux, in a pamphlet extolling the ideals of 'The New Soldiery', expressed the hope that they would convert excommunicated knights and seek out from among the 'rogues and impious men, robbers and committers of sacrilege, murderers, perjurers and adulterers', men who, after absolution by their bishop, would devote their fighting abilities to a worthy cause and live within the framework of their monastic rule. There can be little doubt that many of them did (on the surface at least) effect this change, but inevitably as the Templars grew richer so they became a law to themselves. This was even further strengthened by the fact that the most important privilege of the Order was their immunity from sentences of excommunication pronouced by outside bishops or priests.

The great advantage of the Templars to the Kings of Jerusalem was that they provided a steady supply of trained fighting men, resident in the country at all times. Other visiting knights might come and go, but the knights of the Temple were permanently to hand. This great advantage was in the end outweighed by the disadvantage that the Templars would only fight to the orders of their own Grand Master. Furthermore, they were often at variance with two other similar Orders which sprang up in the Holy Land, and in particular with the foremost of these, the Order of St John. The third Order, the last to be founded, that of the Teutonic Knights, followed in its basic principles the rules and regulations established by its two predecessors. Coming, however, somewhat late upon the scene and from Germany, it exerted less influence than the other two Orders which, though international, were predominantly French.

The Order of St John, unlike the Templars who had originally banded together solely as a military arm to defend the pilgrim routes, had its origins in a hospital which had been maintained in Jerusalem even before the capture of the city in 1099. Originally established, it would seem, by merchants from the great trading centre of Amalfi in Italy, the function of the hospital was to provide shelter and assistance to pilgrims and such simple medical aid as was available at the time. While the founder of the Templars had been a knight, Hugh de Payens, the founder of the Order of St John was a monk, Brother Gerard, whose life was dedicated to the care of the poor and the sick. Thus, although at a later date the Templars and the Knights of St John seemed to be equally militant orders, the origin of the latter – and one never entirely forgotten – lay in a hospital and in hospitaller service. During the chaos that followed upon the capture of Jerusalem the small hospice maintained by Gerard was of the greatest value to the army and to the pilgrims who now thronged the city.

From the very beginning, the Hospital, as it was called, enjoyed the favour of the rulers of Jerusalem. Godfrey de Bouillon made it the gift of some land and his example was followed over the years by his successors as rulers of the kingdom, and by others who wanted to record their thanks for the services rendered them by the Hospitallers. Baldwin I, for instance, after a victory over the Egyptians, gave the Order a tenth of the booty, while many rich ecclesiastics throughout the East gave it a

Two Templars share a horse: from Matthew Paris's Historia Major I, *c.1118.*

tithe of their revenue. Gerard's successor, Raymond de Puy, effected a basic change in the Order's structure which was to have an unlooked for effect upon its future. In emulation of the Templars, he grafted upon what had until then been a purely hospitaller service a military arm, designed like the Templars to operate as protectors on the pilgrim routes. But, again as with the Templars, the definition of 'a protector' was elastic. It came in the long run to mean a knight or soldier dedicated to fight against the enemies of the Faith. In 1136 the great castle of Bethgeblin, built by Fulk of Jerusalem to guard the south of Palestine against the Moslems and to keep an eye on the key port of Ascalon, was given to the Order for them to garrison and maintain out of their revenues. It was not, however, until after the middle of the twelfth century that the Order of St John developed almost as markedly a military aspect as the Templars. By this time they already had a number of castles in Syria, largely manned by mercenaries. Many of them were the gift of Count Raymond of Tripoli, who was anxious to have the Hospitallers as his allies against the constant enemy incursions into his lands.

The rise of the great Military Orders, so important a feature of the history of *Outremer*, was a curious example of an amalgamation of religious and secular influences and interests. There can be no doubt, however, that the induction of a new candidate was a highly emotional experience. The novice had to declare that he was not married, nor in

A knight of the Order of St John.

debt, nor subject to any other lord. His family tree and necessary quarterings were investigated before he was interviewed and, if received, he had to promise to live and die in the service of his Order. When an aspiring candidate came for examination the Master or the president of the Chapter asked the other members present if he was considered acceptable, for no one could be received unless there was unanimous assent. In the case of the application of a candidate to join the Order of St John the president addressed him as follows: 'Good friend, you desire the company of the House and you are right in this, for many gentlemen earnestly require the reception of their children or their friends and are most joyful when they can place them in this Order. And if you are willing to be in so excellent and so honourable company and in so holy an Order as that of the Hospital, you are right in this. But if it is because you see us well clothed, riding on great chargers and having everything for our comfort, then you are misled, for when you would desire to eat, it will be necessary for you to fast, and when you would wish to fast, you will have to eat. And when you would desire to

The Great Hall in the Krac des Chevaliers.

sleep, it will be necessary for you to keep watch, and when you would like to stand on watch, you will have to sleep. And you will be sent this side of the sea and beyond, into places which will not please you, and you will have to go there. It will be necessary for you therefore to abandon all your desires to fulfil those of another and to endure other hardships in the Order, more than I can describe to you. Are you willing to suffer all these things?'

It was this insistence upon the all-embracing right that the Orders had to their members' obedience that, comprehensible though it may seem at first sight, was to prove their gravest drawback. It led in Palestine and Syria to a rivalry between the two main Orders that on occasions even led to bloodshed. It led to a rivalry on battle-fields, where both were engaged, in which the glory of one Order above another was set far beyond the overall considerations of tactics. The endless disputes between Templars and Knights of St John led to a serious weakening of the Kingdom of Jerusalem. In the case of the Templars, their power and position finally led to their suppression in the fourteenth century, and to the confiscation of all their lands and possessions at the instigation of Philip of France. But that was after the Holy Land had fallen, and *Outremer* was no more, when the Teutonic Knights turned their activities to the colonisation of pagan Prussia and when the Order of St John became domiciled in Rhodes. All this was in the future. For the moment the shadows of the knights of the Military Orders loom large in the history of the Crusades.

The greatest contribution that the knights made to the kingdoms of the East lay in the sphere of military architecture. Being at the most little more than a few thousand men in command of mercenaries and irregulars, the knights had of necessity to perfect the castle; the shelter within which a relative handful of men could hold at bay large armies, and inflict such damage on their attackers as to make a siege so expensive as to be impractical. In essence, the castle, such as had been introduced by the Normans into England during the Conquest to hold down the land, was an earthmound of circular shape, surrounded by a dry ditch. Flattened at the top to form a defence point, the mound was surrounded by a wooden palisade. Such a simple rallying point and protective shelter was perfectly adequate under English conditions, and against relatively untrained peasantry armed with simple weapons such as bows and spears. Logically enough, the wooden palisade was next converted into a stone wall, and stone buildings were erected inside it and on the

Opposite: *The Chapel of the Krac des Chevaliers.*

mound itself. In some parts of the country, where some dominant hill or rocky outcrop presented itself, the Norman architects had to do little more than improve upon the natural position.

In the East the Crusaders found fortifications already erected by Byzantines and Moslems, many of them on the sites which had naturally suggested themselves over the centuries – long indeed before even the Romans had involved themselves in the affairs of Syria and Palestine. Basically the style of Crusader castles followed that of western Europe, being a graft of western upon eastern styles of fortification. Unlike the castles of nobles in Europe, however, they were barracks rather than fortified family houses. The garrisons were relieved, circumstances permitting, at regular intervals. Fresh knights and the troops came to do their tour of duty while their predecessors went back to the comforts of Tripoli or Antioch or Jerusalem. They were, as T E Lawrence described them in his study of Crusader castles, sometimes 'massive and unsubtle'. Referring to the famous Castle Pilgrim at Athlit (whose remains can still be seen), he remarked of it that 'such a place is as much a prison for its defenders as a refuge . . .' On the realistic side, however, it must be said that Castle Pilgrim survived a six-month attack in 1220, and was only finally lost in 1291 because there were insufficient men to garrison it.

The principal advance in military architecture was the use of towers to flank the long curtain walls. These provided covering-fire to the line of a wall if it was under attack by sappers or miners or battering rams. It was not yet the age of gunpowder, and such relatively simple manual attacks upon fortified positions had changed little since the days of the Romans and the Greeks. In Europe, the single defence line which had evolved from the simple stake palisade was still considered sufficient protection. But in the East, where besiegers, whether Arab, Tatar, or Turk, might be expected to throw thousands of men almost regardlessly at the defences, it did not take long to see that castles needed to be a good deal more elaborate.

The first recourse was to the construction of an inner line concentric with the outer, so that if the besieger should burst the first wall the defenders could retreat within the second, and the whole labour of mining, sapping, siege towers, and siege engines had to be brought into action once again. At points where it seemed as if the enemy was about to break through the inner ring the defenders would once again narrow their defences and, with the rubble and broken masonry to hand, construct yet another interior counterwall. The final refuge of all was the keep, usually a tower slightly larger than all the others, and serving as a command post throughout the siege. Sometimes the keep was built at a salient point as part of the enceinte itself, while at others it was built completely separately – a castle within a castle.

Wherever possible, Crusader castles were built on a base of solid rock, so that the activities of sappers and miners were made that much more difficult. Krak des Chevaliers, for instance, that impressive masterpiece of the Order of St John was built in such a way, rising upwards in concentric form. It was only taken in 1272 because, like Castle Pilgrim, there was insufficient money and not enough men to garrison it properly. Manpower was always the dominating factor. As J Quentin Hughes puts it in *Fortress*: 'Because of the shortage of manpower impregnable sites had to be chosen and exploited. Strong keeps built after the manner of the French castles became a feature of these fortresses, and concentric rings of defences, built one inside the other and rising higher and higher were constructed, so that those defending the outer walls were covered by fire from positions behind and above them.' The words 'castles and Crusaders' are inextricably bound together in the imagination. It was so in fact. Without castles the Crusaders and particularly the Military Orders would never have been able to hold the land.

Seal of the Templars, the 'poor knights of Christ'.

The Moslem Tide

The essential founder of the Moslem revival was undoubtedly the Syrian ruler, Nur-ed-Din. He achieved one of his greatest political successes in 1154 by overthrowing the ruler of Damascus and seizing the city. The independence of Damascus, which had been largely secured through its alliance with the Latins, was now at an end and a further threat to their continued existence had emerged. In the absence of any hope of further help from Europe, the King of Jerusalem, Baldwin III, wisely decided to renew friendly relations with Constantinople. The Byzantine Emperor Manuel acquired the suzerainty of Antioch, while Baldwin married the Emperor's niece. The aim and objective of these manoeuvres, on the part of the Latins, was to weaken the power of Nur-ed-Din. Manuel, however, had his own objectives in Asia and elsewhere, and he was not prepared to sacrifice them in order to save the position of the Kingdom of Jerusalem.

From 1162, when Baldwin III was succeeded by his brother Amaury, the real issue in the East was concerned with the fate of Egypt. The richest country of all—Napoleon was later to refer to it as 'the most important in the world'—Egypt had been ruled for some two hundred years by the Fatimite Caliphs who, by the mid-twelfth century, had lost practically all control over the land. Civil war, constant riots, and what amounted in effect to the rule of a succession of Viziers or chief ministers, had made it clear to Latins and Syrian Moslems alike that Egypt was ripe for a change of regime. Nur-ed-Din's empire now extended from Kurdistan to the borders of Egypt. Only the divided Franks lay between him and this ultimate prize. He had raided Antioch and Tripoli, and his brilliant and remarkable lieutenant, Saladin, had by 1171 become virtually King of Egypt.

Opposite: *Persian portrait presumed to be of Saladin, c.1180.*

Nur-ed-Din was, in fact, on the verge of invading Egypt to deprive Saladin of the immense spoils of the Fatimites when he died. At almost the same time the death of Amaury deprived the Kingdom of Jerusalem of a firm and politically perspicacious ruler, leaving on the throne a thirteen-year-old son, Baldwin IV. The latter was highly intelligent, one of the finest characters of his time, a youth who had been well educated by the historian William of Tyre, and who might well have revived the fortunes of the Latins in the East but for one tragic defect. Already, by the time that he was crowned, it was clear that he had contracted leprosy.

Saladin, although he may have owed something to the happy fortune which left him unchallenged in the East, was without any doubt the most brilliant soldier and administrator of his time. Born in 1138, Salah-ed-Din, 'Honour of the Faith', was a Kurd from Armenia, and he retained to the end of his days something of the endurance and integrity of these mountain people. Educated at Damascus, ever a great city of Moslem learning, he had been chosen by the Fatimid Caliph of Egypt, when he was only thirty, as the Vizier of Egypt. This was an anomalous position since he was the lieutenant of an orthodox (Sunnite) king, Nur-ed-Din, yet he was now serving as what amounts to the prime minister of a heretical (Shiite) Caliph. Quite apart from learning how to walk delicately between these two masters, Saladin also had many troubles to deal with in Egypt itself; involving a struggle with the Sudanese that lasted for some six years.

His most serious test, however, arose when the Latins under King Amaury, realising that Palestine was now trapped between Nur-ed-Din's Syria to the north and his lieutenant Saladin's Egypt to the south, organised a combined operation in company with the Byzantines. Their object was to capture the important harbour of Damietta on the Pelusiac branch of the Nile. 'The harbours of Damietta and Alexandria', as Stanley Lane-Poole wrote in a biography of Saladin, 'gave the Moslems the command of a fleet, and enabled them to cut off the communications of the Crusaders with Europe, stop the annual pilgrim ships, and seize their supplies. Every effort must be made to break this fatal chain, which threatened the very existence of the Latin power in Palestine . . .' Unfortunately for Amaury, the Byzantine fleet was delayed by head winds and, when the siege of Damietta opened in November 1169, Saladin had had time to strengthen the city's defences and bring up thousands of troops. The investing army ran short of food, winter rains swelled the Nile and flooded their camp, and the whole venture expired in failure. In the following year Saladin took the initiative, attacked Gaza and plundered it, and seized Aila at the head of the Gulf of Aqaba.

Saladin's ability in war, coupled with his determination to expel the Franks from Palestine, served to reconcile the divergent parties of Islam. Sunnites and Shiites were prepared, temporarily at least, to forget their differences when they saw the rich profit that was to be had under the command of Saladin. Even Egyptians and Turks were willing to enlist in the same company under his banner. With Saladin the concept of the Holy War against the infidel became something meaningful. As W F Knox wrote of him: 'The opportunity of Saladin lay therefore in the fact that his lifetime covers the period when there was a conscious demand for political union in the defence of the Moslem faith'. Educated at Damascus, that great centre of Moslem learning, he was a devout Mohammedan, capable of extremes of emotions and of outstanding courage. Honest and chivalrous, prepared to extend fair treatment to prisoners (with the sole exception of the Templars and the Knights of St John, whom he recognised as implacable enemies) Saladin was a character of rare distinction in his day. Indeed, he would have been remarkable in any age. 'Other virtues', to quote W F Knox again, 'were all his own, his extreme gentleness, his love for children, his flawless honesty, his invariable kindness, his chvalry to women and the weak . . . ' His strength lay above all in his burning and passionate faith. He was determined to rid the East of these deluded Christ-believers, and to hurl the Latin kingdom into the sea. 'Let us purge the air', he said, 'of the very air they breathe.'

On the death of Nur-ed-Din, with Egypt secure behind him, Saladin set about the systematic conquest of Syria where Nur-ed-Din's vassals had rebelled against his young heir, Is-Salih. On the pretext of coming to his aid Saladin moved north, entering Damascus, Emesa and Hamah in 1174. In the following year Baalbek and the area around Aleppo fell to his arms. He was proclaimed Sultan by the Caliph. By 1186 the Latin kingdom was enclosed by Syria in the north, Mosul in the east, and Egypt to the south. Saladin had created a Moslem empire that was dedicated to the expulsion of the Christians. Yet even at this moment he was prepared to make terms with the Latin kingdom, being perfectly well aware that the rivalry of the various factions within it would probably lead to its downfall without much assistance from him. As a Christian historian was later to write of the absurd internecine feuds of the two great Orders: 'Oh ancient treachery of the Temple! Oh long-standing sedition of the Hospitallers!'

A four years' truce, which had been concluded between Saladin and the Latin kingdom, was broken in 1187. Two years before this Baldwin

IV, the leper king who, despite the constant agony of his body, had ruled with wisdom and authority, died in Jerusalem. Since his successor, Baldwin V, was only a child, the kingdom came under the regency of Raymond of Tripoli. It was clearly to everybody's advantage that the truce with Saladin should be carefully observed but, as so often in the affairs of the Latins, it was impossible to control the headstrong ambitions of individual nobles. It was Reginald of Châtillon, Lord of Montreal, who, by breaking the truce, provided Saladin with a fully justifiable reason for war. Reginald had himself sworn to keep the peace but he had not been able to resist ambushing a large Moslem caravan. He refused to surrender the plunder, and imprisoned all the travellers in the dungeons of Krak. Saladin had probably been expecting some such anarchic stupidity on the part of the Latins. He could control his own subjects and ensure their obedience, but these dissident infidels had no such discipline amongst them. His third period of conquest now began.

Troops were summoned from Egypt, feudatories from Syria and Gezira, and the whole of Saladin's empire was put on a war footing. Prior to this he had given the Franks every chance to surrender the booty from the caravan and apologise for their action, but Reginald of Châtillon was not prepared to take orders from the new King of Jerusalem, Guy de Lusignan (Baldwin V had died while still a child). In the summer of 1187 Saladin reviewed his troops. Now, with an army of 20,000 men, 1200 being his formidable cavalry, he prepared to take the offensive on a major scale. On 1 July, 1187, he crossed the Jordan and

Saracen horsemen: from Marinus Sanutus's Handbook for Crusaders, *c.1321.*

moved against the Christian enemy. Part of the army was despatched to Tiberias, where a body of Templars and Hospitallers were cut to pieces. The castle of Tiberias managed, however, to hold out under the command of Eschiva, Countess of Tripoli. (It is noticeable throughout the history of the Latin kingdom that the women regularly showed every whit as much spirit as their men.) Saladin, whose history shows that he was rarely willing to waste much time on besieging fortified places – wisely preferring to march round them and let them fall in due course – decided on this occasion to encamp in front of the castle. He had a feeling that the Christians would not leave it to its fate. The main body of the army was despatched into the hills that lay around. The castle lay, as it were, like bait surrounded by the Moslem army.

Saladin was not mistaken in his belief that the Christians would fall into the trap. They were alarmed enough by his invasion of their land, and were determined to have him back across the Jordan as quickly as possible. Contingents from the Templars and Hospitallers, as well as others from Tripoli and Antioch, were already rallying to form a united Christian army. It was more than clear that the whole safety of the kingdom was at stake. So great was the alarm that the Patriarch of Jerusalem had even sent the relic of the True Cross (discovered in the fourth century) to act as inspiration to all the Christians in their hour of need. King Guy, Raymond of Tripoli (who hated each other), and Reginald of Châtillon, the direct cause of the trouble, were the principal leaders of a combined force which numbered some 1,300 knights, 4,000 mounted sergeants, a similar number of foot soldiers, and a detachment of locally-recruited mounted bowmen.

A great debate was held among the Latins as to their plan of campaign. Raymond, whose wife was besieged in Tiberias, was quite logical. He was confident in the ability of the castle to hold out, stated quite clearly that Tiberias was in any case his personal concern, and added that it was far better to lose Tiberias than to lose the whole country. 'If we advance from here', he added, 'all is lost'. *Here* was Sephoria, fifteen miles away from Tiberias. It was fifteen miles composed of nothing but hill-country where there was not a single spring or well with which to refresh themselves or their horses. Sephoria, on the other hand, was comparatively well-watered. It would be better for the army to wait there and let Saladin make the first move. It was the month of July, a time of desolate, searing heat in that land. Raymond, who knew it better than most, was wise to advise the King and Reginald of Châtillon to stay where they were. Unfortunately for the army, unfortunately for the fate of the Latin kingdom of the East, Guy de Lusignan was persuaded that the essential thing was to relieve Tiberias at once. The decision was taken – a fatal one – to advance across the barren land and confront Saladin.

At dawn on 3 July, 1187, the army broke camp and left Sephoria. Under the blazing eye of the midsummer sun the armoured knights, their white surcoats scarcely disseminating the heat of their mail, let alone of the quilted jackets beneath them, sweated onward through that dusty, treeless land. Saladin, hearing that the Christians had left Sephoria and were coming to meet him, remarked drily, 'Exactly what I wanted!' He had lured his enemies into a death trap.

There was no water on the way, and men and horses were both suffering terribly long before evening brought them some respite. They encamped for the night where a rocky hill with two summits lifted above the village of Hattin, where there was a green valley and a lake. It was this thought that had lured them on, but they were too exhausted to reach it before nightfall. Saladin and his troops, in any case, had already occupied the area in front of them. When dawn came the Christians, who had listened all night to the sounds and songs of the Moslem army, found that they were surrounded. They would never reach the water. Saladin, to increase the hopelessness of their position, had his troops set fire to the sun-burned grasses around the hill. Out of the smoke, out of the parched land which had already begun to waver with heat, the mounted archers stormed upon them.

The knights delivered charge after charge, but all save one of these were beaten back. Raymond of Tripoli, Balian of Ibelin, and Reynald of Sidon together with their followers burst through the Moslem ranks. It was too late for any others to follow them, and the white-robed horsemen let them pass through and then firmly closed their ranks. The Christians were unable to fight their way back to their comrades marooned on the hill. In despair, well aware that this was almost certainly the end of the kingdom, they made their way to the safety of Tripoli. The army rallied round King Guy as they retreated up the hill. Time and again Templars or Hospitallers together with other knights showed their undying courage by charging the advancing horsemen. On the summit of the Horns of Hattin the king's tent and the royal standard marked the last stand of the Christians, Saladin himself never failed to give credit to the bravery of the enemy. Foolish they might have been to fall into his trap, but they never disgraced the code by which they lived. Among the dead was the Bishop of Acre, and in his hands was the relic of the Holy Cross. The crescent had triumphed.

King Guy, Reginald of Châtillon, and other nobles and barons who had survived the final onslaught, horseless and deprived of their weapons, were taken to Saladin's tent. They were received graciously. Saladin made the King sit next to him, and offered him a drink of rose-water, cooled with the snows of Mount Hermon. Guy, having drunk, handed the goblet to Reginald. Saladin could not conceal his fury at the sight of this perjurer, this man who had caused the Moslems so much trouble, and whose capture of the caravan had led to this war. 'Tell the King', he said to an interpreter, 'that it was he not I who offered that man to drink.' By this he meant that, by the code of the Arabs a prisoner's life was safe if one had given him to eat and drink. This he had done to Guy, but not to Reginald. King Guy was to be spared but Saladin had no mercy for Reginald of Châtillon, whose head was struck off. 'Kings do not kill kings,' he said reassuringly to Guy, who no doubt expected that the same fate awaited him, 'but that man's insolence was beyond the bounds of tolerance.' He now gave orders that all the other nobles were to be spared, with the exception of the Templars and the Hospitallers.

Saladin's horsemen: from Romans de Godefroi de Bouillon et de Salehadin, *c.1337.*

All of these were formally executed by Moslem *sufis*, men of religion whose devotion to their cause was as fanatical as that of the members of the Military Orders. As for the rank and file, Saladin's clemency could not be expected to extend to them. They were destined to be sold into slavery.

The battle of the Horns of Hattin determined the fate of the Latin kingdom. The East was Saladin's. Nearly every available Latin male had reported for duty in the army that King Guy had led on its disastrous march from Sephoria. Something like half of them were slaughtered while the others were either enslaved or, if noble, held as prisoners. Tiberias surrendered, the countess being chivalrously escorted by Saladin's men to the safety of Tripoli. Nothing now remained but for Saladin to proceed to the occupation of all the ports, cities, and fortresses of *Outremer*. The ports were first and foremost on the list. Sagacious in this as in all else, he realised that his victory at Hattin must almost inevitably raise a storm in Europe: that he might expect a fresh Crusade to set out to liberate the Holy Land. There could be no doubt in Saladin's mind, or in any other's, that Jerusalem must shortly fall before the sword of the all-conquering ruler of the Moslem world.

The Battle of the Horns of Hattin: from Matthew Paris's Historia Major I.

Aftermath

Saladin's march through Palestine was in the nature of a triumphal procession. Within two months almost the whole of the land, from Beirut in the north to Gaza in the south, had fallen to the arms of the man who had succeeded in uniting Islam. It was little short of ninety years since the army of the First Crusade had first entered the Holy Land, and now all that had been achieved – or had seemed to have been achieved – was irretrievably lost. A few castles held by the Military Orders, the great city of Tyre, and Jerusalem itself, these were all that remained of the Latin kingdom in the East.

Saladin was determined to give his enemies no chance of rallying, or of receiving reinforcements from Europe. Within four days of his victory at Hattin his army was encamped before the walls of Acre. The city surrendered to him on 8 July, on the condition that the lives and property of its inhabitants were guaranteed. Saladin's brother Al-Adil had, in the meantime, moved up from Egypt, besieging and taking Jaffa. Inland, Nazareth and Sephoria were occupied, while other detachments of Saladin's army had entered Caesarea and Haifa. On 4 September Ascalon fell, Saladin receiving envoys from Jerusalem during the darkness that accompanied an eclipse of the sun. Those Christians who had heard of the eclipse of the moon, which had heralded the First Crusade on its triumphal way to the capture of the Holy City, may have decried the sinister omen.

On 20 September, 1187, Saladin began the siege of Jerusalem. The defence of the city was in the hands of Balian of Ibelin, one of the leading barons who had fought their way through the encircling Moslems at the Horns of Hattin. He was a man whom Saladin respected as a worthy and honourable foe. From the very start, Balian was faced with the impossibility of adequately defending a city where there were no others of his calibre – only two knights, it is said – and few enough men-at-arms to form a garrison-force capable of covering the circuit of the walls. Yet, even with the inadequate resources at his disposal, Balian refused to give up the Holy City without a fight. It was nine days before Saladin's sappers had opened a large enough breach near the Gate of the Column for any assault to be successful. On 30 September, Balian came before Saladin and asked him for terms of the city's surrender. 'Had you opened the gates to me at the beginning,' said the Sultan, 'I would have considered terms, but now I have taken an oath that nothing but unconditional surrender will suffice.' He went on to remind Balian of the treatment that had been meted out to the Moslems when the army of the First Crusade had captured the city—why should he act so differently? Balian's reply to this was that if the Christians saw that their situation was quite hopeless they would first of all kill their women and children, and then they would destroy all the Moslem holy places and massacre the Moslem population. After this, they would sally out and die to a man. Saladin, naturally enough, had no desire to enter a Jerusalem running with the blood of his own people, and where all the shrines sacred to Islam had been destroyed. He agreed upon a ransom fee, ten dinars a man, five for a woman and one for a child. Balian pointed out that the rich could afford these terms but that there were twenty thousand poor people in the city who could never raise the money—would Saladin agree to a lump-sum for all of them? This was fixed at 30,000 dinars, for which seven thousand poor would be ransomed but the rest sold into slavery. Later, at the request of Saladin's brother, a further thousand were released, and a further five hundred as a gesture of respect to Balian. On 2 October, Saladin entered Jerusalem.

All was in marked distinction from the scenes of carnage, rape and looting which had marked the entry of the Crusaders into the city eighty-eight years before. Saladin's men were under strict discipline, something which, if the Normans had ever been able to achieve it, might have permanently secured for them their occupation of the Holy Land. Sentries were posted outside the principal shrines of Christian, Moslem, and Jew, while organised pickets patrolled the streets to ensure that the peace was kept and that no one was molested.

Sir John Glubb comments in *The Lost Centuries*: 'The principal explanation [for the humane treatment of the conquered] lies undoubtedly in the fact that the Arabs in 1187 were a civilised people, while the Franks in 1099 were not. There were, however, other reasons which may also have influenced Saladin. Further fighting would have resulted in the death of many more Muslims and in the partial destruction of the city, which was holy to the Muslims as well as to the Christians . . . ' It remains nevertheless to the eternal credit of this great Sultan that, in the moment of victory, he behaved in a manner to which every Christian – if the adjective was to have any meaning at all – should have aspired.

Saladin's next objective was the great seaport of Tyre. As long as this remained open to the Christians, reinforcements could reach them from Europe – and he accurately anticipated that the capture of Jerusalem could only lead to a further Crusade. He was to some extent forestalled. Shortly after the battle at Hattin, Conrad of Montferrat and a company of knights had reached the city, while a number of refugee barons and their men had also sought shelter there. Tyre, connected with the mainland only by a sandy isthmus across which ran a great wall, was one of the strongest cities in the Mediterranean. Saladin, who was ever averse to protracted sieges, did in fact spend nearly six weeks encamped before Tyre, but the onset of winter and the failure of an Egyptian blockade by sea convinced him that Tyre, for the moment at least, was best left alone. In this he made the only mistake of his remarkable campaign. The city, as he had himself foreseen, was to prove the spearhead for a further Latin assault upon the land of Palestine.

As soon as the news reached Europe the papacy immediately set about promoting a new Crusade. Unlike the previous ones, however, the Third Crusade was very largely promoted by the lay power. The three powerful monarchs of Germany, France, and England were primarily responsible. Foremost of these was Frederick Barbarossa of Germany, a fine soldier and statesman, and a man who knew the terrain from having taken part in the Second Crusade. Philip Augustus of France and Henry II of England, despite the bad blood between them, managed to achieve sufficient reconciliation to agree on an Anglo-French campaign. To provide money for this a 'Saladin tithe' was levied on all those who did not take the Cross. This may well have led to a number of tax-dodgers joining the army, but it also provided a useful capital sum from the many merchants and others who were unwilling to have their business pursuits disturbed. Sir Ernest Barker commented that: 'Thousands must have joined the Third Crusade in order to escape paying either their taxes or the interest on their debts; and the atmosphere of the gold-digger's camp . . . must have begun more than ever to characterize the crusading armies. The lay basis of the Third Crusade made it, in one sense, the greatest of all Crusades, in which all the three great monarchs of western Europe participated; but it also made it a failure, for the kings of France and England carried their political rivalries into the movement, in which it had been agreed that they should be sunk.' By the time that the Anglo-French enterprise got under way Henry II would in any case have died. His place as King of England was taken by Richard I, the Lion Heart.

The Crusade can be seen as having had three leaders but all had the same objective: first of all, Acre, and then moving on from there the recapture of the Holy Land and Jerusalem. As far as Frederick was concerned, the approach of the German army by the overland route was complicated by the hostility of the Byzantine Emperor, Isaac II. Isaac, who was being hard pressed by the Seljuk Sultan of Iconium, had been forced to conclude a treaty with Saladin, so as to relieve the pressure on the borders of Byzantium. Frederick wisely avoided taking his army via Constantinople – there had been clashes already between his troops and the Byzantines – and crossed into Asia and Gallipoli in March 1190. The Anglo-French army, whose alliance had been determined, on the surface at least, between Philip and Richard I in a new agreement, spent the winter of 1190-1 in uneasy inactivity in Sicily. There was never any love lost between the English and the French. It would hardly be inaccurate to say that the basic aims and ambitions of the Crusade were lost sight of in the scarcely concealed animosity of the monarchs, and the unconcealed dislike for one another of their troops. As the history of the Latin kingdom of the Holy Land itself had shown, political and power rivalries were fatal to the European cause.

It took nearly three years from the disaster at Hattin for the armies to assemble. What was left to the Franks in Palesine – principally Tyre and Tripoli – was only held by the intervention of King William of Sicily, private individuals like James of Avesnes from Flanders, and a strong naval force from Flanders and Denmark, as well as a flotilla of

Frederick Barbarossa drowns in 1190: from a German manuscript, c.1250.

Top left *Henry II;* top right *Richard I;* bottom left *John;* bottom right
Henry III; from Chronicle of Kings, *early fourteenth-century manuscript.*

ships from London. In the long story of the Crusades it is always important to remember that the process of involvement in the Levant was a continuous one. The highlights are well known, but it was the steady flow of men, money and arms into the disputed area that made any Latin kingdom in that hostile region even remotely possible.

As forerunner of the help that was on its way from Europe the magnificent German army of about 40,000 men was already marching through the territory of the Seljuk Sultan, Kilij Arslan, whose son was defeated near Iconium, the city falling into Frederick's hands. So great was the fear that the Emperor's name inspired, and so formidable from all reports did his army seem to be, that Saladin summoned all his vassals. He sent a proclamation to the faithful that they must join him immediately in order to ward off the threat that was presented by the Germans marching through Asia, and the English and French who were expected at any moment by sea. It is probable enough that the European combination would have been more than even the Islam that Saladin had united could have dealt with. Fate was on the side of the Moslems. During the fording of a river in the plain of Seleucia, Frederick Barbarossa was accidentally drowned. The loss of so great a leader would have been demoralising to any army, but to the Germans – ever prone to hero-worship – the loss of a figure who had become a legend in his lifetime was disastrous. Despite the valiant efforts of his son Frederick, the Duke of Swabia, to restore morale the German army gradually disintegrated. Frederick reached Acre by sea in October 1190, accompanied by only a relative handful of what had probably been the finest armed force ever to set out for the Holy Land. One Arabic historian goes so far as to say that it was only the death of Frederick Barbarossa that saved the Moslems from losing both Syria and Palestine, and even Egypt as well.

The main event during the immediate years after the fall of Jerusalem, and the arrival of the Crusading armies from Europe, was the siege of Acre. Saladin, who had released Guy of Lusignan, former King of Jerusalem, from imprisonment on the understanding that he would never take up arms again against the Moslems, was to be disappointed in his trust. Guy, having mustered some 200 knights from Sicily who had been instrumental in saving Tripoli for the Latins, broke his oath and led them south to Acre. He was accompanied along the coast by ships from Pisa and Sicily, who were as eager to trade as they were to promote the Christian cause. Having laid siege to Acre, Guy and his small force were in their turn besieged by Saladin. There followed a long drawn-out campaign which was somewhat akin to twentieth-century trench warfare. It lasted right through the autumn and winter of 1189 and the whole year of 1190. The situation was to be further complicated by the fact that Guy, who still laid claim to the crown of Jerusalem, was challenged by Conrad of Montferrat, whose own claim was largely based on the fact that it was he who had so far preserved the all-important city of Tyre. Conrad's position was reinforced by his marriage to Isabella, the younger sister of Guy's deceased wife, which gave him the right to the title through his position as the consort of the Queen of Jerusalem. Thus, at the moment when the besieging Latins around Acre were in a desperate position through lack of food and supplies, and when relief from Europe had not yet reached the Holy Land, the Kingdom (such of it as yet remained) was in dispute between two rival kings. 'Whom God wishes to destroy he first drives mad' – the old saying certainly had more than a little relevance to the affairs of Europeans in the Holy Land.

Unusually fortunate Crusaders are released by the Saracens : from Matthew Paris's Historia Major II, *c.1240.*

ti prile. et comment li rois phos re
tourna en france pour sa maladie z pour
la doubte de la maison du roi richart.

Acre and After

The arrival of Frederick, Duke of Swabia, in October 1190 served to raise the spirits of the besiegers of Acre. Small though the number of men that he brought with him, the presence of Barbarossa's son, and the knowledge that he represented only the spearhead of European reinforcements, proved sufficient encouragement for the Latins to insist on an action against Saladin's advance guard – an action which proved inconclusive but suggested at any rate that an aggressive spirit had now been infused into the army. Efforts were redoubled to undermine and batter down the walls. 'For the first time they employed a battering ram (an indication that the Moslem garrison had become enfeebled enough to allow the Crusaders to get to close quarters) . . . It was a huge beam with an iron head which weighed nearly three hundred-weight, and had been constructed at great expense by the Archbishop of Besançon'. The combined efforts of the men operating this ram, together with another called the 'cat', both protected under penthouses or 'sows', reduced part of the walls. The mass assault which followed was a failure, the besieged proving that they had only been lying quiet until the time came for them to show their strength. Beaten back yet again, the Christians might well have lost heart but for the fact that at this moment an English fleet reached Tyre bringing men, stores, and money, and having aboard such prestigious figures as Baldwin, Archbishop of Canterbury, and Hubert, Bishop of Salisbury. They brought with them also the more than welcome news that Philip of France and Richard of England were indeed on their way.

The chaplain to the Archbishop, who was among those who visited the Latin camp, gives a sorry picture of the state to which the besiegers had been reduced by the long months in trenches. 'We found our army –

Opposite: *Richard the Lion Heart reaches Acre : thirteenth-century manuscript.*

153

I say it with grief and lamentation – given up to shameful behaviour, and yielding to ease and lust rather than practising virtue. The Lord is not in the camp; there is none that doeth good . . . '

It was the same complaint that had been made over and over again during the past decades: something seemed to happen to the hardy Normans and men of western Europe when they spent too long in the indolent East. 'The chiefs envy one another, and fight over privilege. The lesser folk are in want and are not helped. There is neither chastity, sobriety or faith in the camp, nor charity . . . The enemy are besieging us, and challenge us daily and persist in attacking us, while our knights, for their part, lie skulking within their tents.'

At the same time, all was not entirely well with the Moslem troops, and the great Saladin himself was often ill with fever. The winter of 1190 with its cold and rain was a dispiriting one for both sides. The spring of 1191 saw a great change in this war which had practically reached the point of stalemate. On 20 April Philip of France landed at Acre to be followed seven weeks later by Richard I. It had taken almost four years for the principal protagonists of the West to reach the battlefield. Even allowing for the difficulties of communication, transportation, and logistics in the twelfth century, the relief of Acre and of Palestine should have been accomplished in half the time.

The Romans had run an empire based on foot-soldiers and sailing ships, and had been able to move whole armies within a matter of months from one end of the Mediterranean to the other. The Romans, however, were guided in the main by a central purpose, by directives issued from Rome. In the fractured Europe of this period, where new nationalisms bedevilled most issues, there was no longer any central control. The papacy had for a time assumed it, and had for a period even managed to impose it, but the unifying message of Roman Christianity no longer obtained among the rulers of western Europe. King Richard, for instance, after his many disagreements with Philip of France, had gone so far astray from the principal object of the Crusade as to turn aside and seize Cyprus.

It is possible that this diversion was not entirely selfishly haphazard, as some historians have seen it. On the surface of it, Richard seized Cyprus from Isaac Comnenus, a prince of the Comneni dynasty who had been dispossessed of the throne of Byzantium. In Cyprus at the small port of Limassol he had also married Berengaria of Navarre. His capture of Cyprus, however, may well have been dictated by the very real assets that so large and fertile an island presented as a base for victualling the troops engaged in the Holy Land. It is not insignificant that, while he was engaged in the short campaign which gave him the island, Richard was visited by Guy de Lusignan. The latter naturally acquainted him with the desperate situation – principally shortage of food – in which the besiegers of Acre found themselves. Cyprus, only one hundred miles away from the seaboard of Syria, was an ideal solution to their problems. Richard subsequently sold the island to Guy de Lusignan who established a dynasty there. Cyprus was, in fact, to provide the Latins with a secure base in the eastern Mediterranean for three centuries, long after the Kingdom of Jerusalem had finally and forever fallen.

'And so,' runs *The Itinerary of King Richard*, 'having concluded these matters Richard straightway turned his thoughts towards his passage; and, when he had arranged his baggage, set sail with a favourable wind...' Richard took passage in a large galley from Famagusta, uneasily aware of the rumour that Acre had already fallen, which would mean that all the glory of bringing the siege to a successful conclusion would belong to his rival, Philip of France. The French had indeed already attempted an assault in the first week of June, but had been driven off by Saladin's men attacking them from the east. Richard meanwhile engaged in a successful action against a large Moslem ship, which was bound for Acre with stores and reinforcements. 'After destroying this ship, the king and all his company hastened with joy and eagerness towards Acre, where he longed to be. Thanks to a favourable wind on the very next night his fleet cast anchor off Tyre . . . Acre was then girt round on every side by an infinite number of people from every Christian nation under heaven . . . Beyond them lay an innumerable army of Turks (not Turks alone, but Moslems of every race) swarming on the mountains and valleys, the hills, and the plains, and having their tents, bright with coloured devices of all kinds, pitched everywhere. Our men could also see Saladin's pair of lions and those of his brother, and Takadin the champion of heathendom. Saladin himself was keeping a watch on the sea-coasts without however ceasing to contrive frequent and fierce attacks upon the Christians. King Richard too, looking forth, reckoned up the number of his foes; and as he reached the harbour the king of France, together with the chiefs of the whole army, all the lords and mighty men, welcomed him with joy and exultation; for they had long been very eager for him to arrive. It was on the Saturday before the feast of the blessed Barnabas, in Pentecost week (8 June), that King Richard with his followers reached Acre. On his arrival the whole land was stirred with the exultation of the Christians. All the people were in transports of joy, shouting out congratulations and blowing trumpets. He was

brought ashore amid great jubilation; and there was joy because the
desired of all nations had come . . . '

The attacks on the walls of Acre were redoubled, both Philip and
Richard taking a personal hand in directing the sapping operations and
in siting the mangonels. 'King Richard had made two other new sling-
stones of remarkable material and workmanship, and these hit the mark
at an incredible distance. He had also built an engine of the strongest
construction of beams. It had steps fitted to it for getting up, and was
commonly known as the belfry . . . [Nevertheless] Acre seemed a very
hard city to take, not only because of the natural strength of its position,
but also because it was defended by the very choicest Turkish troops . . .
It was all to no purpose that the French had spent so much pains on
constructing engines of war and implements for pulling down the walls;
because the Turks by a sudden volley of Greek fire would destroy
everything their enemies had prepared, no matter at what expense, and
consume it utterly with fire . . . '

Saladin, despite his fever – a sickness from which both Philip and
Richard suffered almost equally – was constantly with his troops in-
spiring fresh attacks on the besieging forces. He also called up new levies
from all over his empire. The siege of Acre was distinguished by the
presence not only of three kings of men, with all their most important
followers and lesser nobles, but by innumerable actions of fire and
spirit. '. . . Meanwhile the King of France's diggers gradually burrowing
by subterranean passages reached the very foundations of the walls and
filled the chasm they had made with logs to which they set fire. Then,
when the fire had consumed the beams upholding the wall, a great part
of it gave way. Very many Christians ran up to this spot in the hope of
entering, whilst the Turks came up to drive them back. Oh! how many
banners might you then see and devices of many a shape, not to mention
the desperate (valour) of the Turks as they hurled Greek fire against our
men.'

On Richard's orders a kind of shed was built under whose shelter the
most skilful cross-bowmen were able to keep up a relentless fire against
the men manning the walls. 'To hearten his own men for the combat and
to dispirit the Saracens by his presence, he had himself carried there on
silken cushions. From this position he worked a crossbow, in the manage-
ment of which he was very skilful, and slew many of the foes by the bolts
that he discharged.' On another occasion, when Richard's sappers had
fired a tunnel under the wall, causing part of it to collapse, a general
attack was launched. '. . . Our men-at-arms in their greed for fame and
victory, began to don their arms. Amongst the banners of these were

the Earl of Leicester; that of Andrew de Chavigny and of Hugh Brown. The Bishop of Salisbury also came up, equipped in the noblest fashion, and many more. . . . The Turkish warriors, hurriedly seizing their arms, came thronging up and flung themselves upon their assailants. The men-at-arms strove to get in; the Turks to hurl them back. Rolled together in a confused mass they fought at close quarters, hand against hand, and sword against sword . . . Never has there been such a people as these Turks for their prowess in war.'

Shortly after this engagement the defenders of Acre shouted down and asked for terms for surrender. King Richard, a politician as well as a soldier, had already been in touch with Saladin, but the latter was unwilling to abandon Acre. In any case, the Crusaders' demand for the restoration of the kingdom as it had been before Hattin was absurd. The two-year siege of Acre ended finally on 11 July, 1191, two hundred thousand gold dinars being the ransom asked for the lives of the garrison, with the additional proviso that nearly two thousand Christians were to be liberated and the relic of the True Cross (lost at the Horns of Hattin) to be restored. Saladin, who had recently received massive reinforcements, and was fairly confident of being able to dislodge the Crusaders, was indignant that the garrison had surrendered without his approval.

Richard the Lion Heart is handed over to Emperor Henry VI in 1192.

However, as a man of honour, he accepted the fact that surrender given by his officers was equivalent to one coming from himself.

Less than a month after the occupation of Acre Philip of France sailed for home. He left behind him, however, the bulk of the French army under the command of Hugh, Duke of Burgundy. Philip, even more than Richard and Saladin, had been seriously ill with fever and he had in any case less stomach for warfare than either of them. Richard was now in overall command of the armies. Whatever the French might feel, he was the dictator of policy, and one of his first acts was to have the Moslem garrison put to death. His action has evoked a horrified response from many historians, who contrast it not unnaturally with the clemency so often showed by Saladin. On the other hand, the latter was far from always clement. When it came to the Templars and Hospitallers, as has been seen, he had no hestitation in having them summarily executed. In his earlier life his treatment of his Moslem opponents in Cairo had shown that he had no mercy if he considered that political expediency was served by cold-blooded murder. Saladin clearly did not hold Richard's action against him as their subsequent friendly relationship was to show.

There can in any case be little doubt that Saladin had been trying to temporise over the payment of the ransom money, hoping that he could spin out the operation until such time as the winter rains put paid to any active campaigning. Two Moslem historians seem to be agreed that the execution of the prisoners was regarded as unavoidable. One pointed out that negotiations about the ransom money had broken down, while the other (Baha-al-Din) said that Saladin refused to pay over the money until the prisoners had first been handed back, and offered further hostages in exchange for the payment of the rest of the gold. Richard, however, who may well have thought that he could fight his way through to Jerusalem while the summer still held, was really the loser. Not only did he fail to obtain the money, but the Christian captives were not released, and the relic of the True Cross – so important to Christian morale – was not returned.

On 25 August, Richard and the army, with the fleet accompanying them, set out by the coast route for Jaffa. Despite constant attacks from the Moslems the march can only be considered a triumphant success. It was evidence of the control and discipline which Richard had managed to impose upon his mixed assortment of troops that, under conditions which had destroyed previous Crusader forces, he managed to keep his force intact and successfully to repulse a major assault at Arsuf. In fact, as Sir Steven Runciman comments: 'The battle of Arsuf was not decisive, but it was a great moral victory for the Christians . . . It was the first great open battle since Hattin, and it showed that Saladin could be defeated. The contemporary poet Ambroise, who was one of Richard's followers, described how a charge of the mounted knights, led by the Templars, proved once again that on suitable terrain (and the battle took place on a plain) nothing could stand against the weight of a heavy cavalry charge. 'These brave men attacked the Turks with so much vigour that every one of them killed his man, drove his lance through his body and lifted him out of the saddle. The Turks (not only Turks, but bedouin Arabs and Sudanese) were completely taken aback for our men struck them like a thunderbolt amid a great cloud of dust. All the foot archers, who had been causing us such losses, had their heads slashed off.'

Saladin in his retreat down the coast adopted a scorched-earth policy, Jaffa being destroyed and Ascalon evacuated. Richard restored the fortifications of Jaffa and halted the army there while he considered the position. The winter had now come on and he had small hope of crossing the Judaean mountains and seizing Jerusalem. In any case, the

Crusaders using a siege-tower : thirteenth-century Spanish manuscript.

strength of his army lay in the mounted knights, who would be at a distinct disadvantage in hilly terrain which was admirably suited to the lightly-armed Arabs and the Turkish bowmen. There can be little doubt that he made the right decision when he decided to forgo the prize of Jerusalem. In any case, had he marched in that direction, he would soon have found that Saladin had cut off his supply route from the sea.

The winter was marked by the seemingly never-ending disputes between the supporters of Guy de Lusignan for the throne of Jerusalem (principally Richard and the English) and the French who for natural reasons preferred the claim of the Duke of Burgundy. It was clear that, since the death of Frederick Barbarossa and the departure of Philip of France, the Crusade, which had in any case been fragmented from the very outset, was unlikely to achieve its main objective. Yet, through the diplomatic negotiations which Richard conducted throughout the following year with Saladin, it can be judged the only successful Latin campaign since the First Crusade.

It is not true, as René Grousset says in his *Histoire des Croisades*, that 'the only object of the Crusade was to recapture Jerusalem.' This had been the emotive object, but the principal one was the re-establishment of the Latin kingdom. The Kingdom of Jerusalem, as such, had already ceased to exist after Hattin. What Richard managed to accomplish was the consolidation of a number of Latin states in the East – something which far outlasted his lifetime. He had added, moreover, to the Christian holdings in the Levant the important and prosperous island of Cyprus. Richard, as both Christian and Moslem accounts reveal, was a first-class soldier, but he was far more than that. He was as able as Saladin himself in those negotiations which mark the statesman. Richard's proposal to Saladin that the latter's brother should marry Joanna, Richard's sister, was evidence that he was prepared to go far further in his dealings with the Moslems than even the 'orientalised' Franks. Joanna refused, just as Al-Adil equally refused to become a Christian in order to marry the lady. But the offer itself was evidence enough that the relationships between Christian and Moslem had completely changed.

The Rape of Byzantium

The one thing that had become evident during the Crusade in which
Richard of England and Saladin were the main protagonists was that the
'Crusading spirit', as it had originally been invoked by Pope Urban II,
was dead. What now animated the Europeans who joined Crusading
banners was political and economic gain. The peace that was signed in
September 1192 was one such as any statesman might have signed. It had
no bearing on the wars of religion. The contested area was neatly
divided: the Latins to keep the coast from north of Tyre to south of
Jaffa, Ascalon to be neutralised, Lydda and Ramlah to be divided
equally, and Christians were to be freely permitted to perform pilgrimages to Jerusalem without any obstruction. The principality of Antioch
and county of Tripoli also remained under the Latins, who thus retained
important bases as well as a number of coastal towns from which, they
hoped, they might one day launch a spearhead attack on Jerusalem.
Saladin, for his part, was reasonably content to have secured the interior.
He had his enemies confined to a narrow strip of land which, though it
could be supplied from the sea, was contained by his forces inland. It
can hardly have escaped his mind either that nothing is potentially more
tenuous and unreliable than sea communications.

Richard I, together with the majority of the Crusaders, embarked for
Europe in the second week of October 1192. Without them, as the Latin
occupants of the land had known well enough, there would in any case
have been no hope of retaining a captured Jerusalem. The forces left
behind were hardly large enough to garrison what remained. The departure of Richard, and the death of Saladin in the following year, marked
the end of the major sequence of engagements between European and
Arab in the East. The conflict between Christian and Moslem was far
from extinguished, but in the future the cause of the Prophet would be
mainly upheld by the Turks, who were to prove as great a threat to

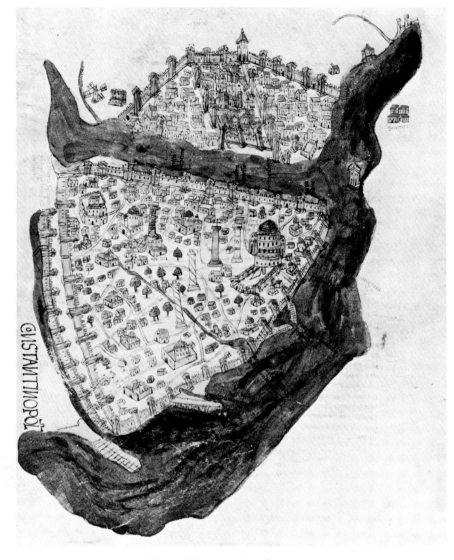

Plan of Constantinople, c.1420.

Europe as the Arabs had been even at the height of their power.

The Fourth Crusade which, unlike its predecessors, was never to come to grips with the Moslem enemy was hatched in France, with the approval of Pope Innocent III. He hoped that it would mark a revival of the Crusading spirit, which had been markedly on the decline since the Second and the Third Crusades. It was intended for Egypt. The Pope hoped that by striking a blow at this most powerful Moslem enemy, the

Crusaders would not only secure the Holy Places but would bring Egypt and its wealth within the orbit of Europe. He hoped also that he would be able to establish Papal ascendancy over the Crusaders, something which, as has been seen, had been noticeably lacking in recent years. In this he was to be disappointed. The temper of the modern nobles was such that they no longer felt themselves subject to Rome as some of their predecessors had been. Their principal objective was, whatever lip-service they might pay to Crusading ideals, the conquest of areas in the East where they might establish feudal kingdoms considerably richer and pleasanter than those they left at home.

The trouble which beset the whole Crusade basically stemmed from the fact that a large fleet was needed. In 1201 Boniface, Marquis of Montferrat in Lombardy, who had been appointed leader of the expedition, set out to confer with the French and German leaders as to the constitution of the army, finances, and objectives. Among those he met was Philip of Swabia, a ruler noted for his dislike of Byzantium and particularly of its present ruler, Alexius III. The former dated from his ancestors who had long been in conflict with the Byzantines over southern Italy and Sicily, and the latter was on account of his being married to Irene Angelina, a Byzantine princess and the daughter of the former Emperor of Constantinople, Isaac. Isaac had been dethroned by Alexius III, imprisoned, and blinded. Philip of Swabia, therefore, had good reason for wanting an attack on Constantinople. He had the motive, and the means were soon put to his hand. His wife's brother, another Alexius, managed to escape from prison in Constantinople and made his way to his sister at the Swabian court. If Philip needed an excuse for a diversion of the Fourth Crusade to Constantinople, and if Boniface was ready to use his position as leader to misdirect it, all was now set for a criminal enterprise that has rarely been surpassed.

In the meantime, ambassadors representing those engaged in the forthcoming Crusade had been in Venice negotiating with the Doge and Council on the all-important question of the transport which was supposedly destined to take them to Egypt and the attack on the Moslems. The Doge of Venice at this time was Enrico Dandolo, aged, blind, but one of the most astute men of his age. He drove a hard bargain with the Crusaders, one which he foresaw could only be to his advantage, for these knights and adventurers from the North were notorious for their inability to pay. The Doge, although for other reasons, also had his eye on Constantinople and the Byzantine Empire. The principal source of Venice's wealth lay in her trade with the East, and the Byzantine Empire with its large oriental connections, its islands spanning the Aegean, and its war galleys and trading fleet had long been a thorn in the side of the Republic. If Venice could lay her hands on those trade routes, on those all-important islands that guarded them, she and she alone would have the monopoly of the Eastern trade. Unbeknown to the Crusaders, who were gradually assembling on Venetian territory throughout 1503, Doge Dandolo and the Council had already signed a treaty with the Sultan of Egypt who, according to one chronicler, 'sent envoys to Venice and told the Venetian that, if he could prevent the Christians attacking his country, he would give them ample reward.' Not only would he pay them a large cash sum, but he would see to it that Venice had advantageous trading concessions at the great port of Alexandria.

It was soon evident that the Crusaders, foolhardy and optimistic, could not possibly pay for the size of fleet which the Doge, acting on his instructions from their leaders, had ordered for them. Many of the Crusaders furthermore had chartered their own shipping and had already made their way independently to *Outremer*. This meant that there was an excess of shipping. The nobles were even reduced to melting down their silver and 'the barons took from each man as much as he could afford to pay'. Even so, they were still far short of the sum required. They were committed to their project, and the only way they could get clear of Venice was to accede to the demands of the Doge. These were simple enough. Venice had a long standing feud with the

Emperor Constantine IX Monomachus : mosaic in Santa Sophia.

city of Zara which belonged to the King of Hungary, and which had long threatened Venice's hegemony of the Adriatic. If the Crusaders were willing to help him in subduing Zara then Dandolo, so he said, was quite convinced that they would secure enough loot to be able to pay their bill. But Zara belonged to a Christian monarch and one of the obligations laid upon all who 'took the Cross' was that they would only fight against the infidel and never against Christians.

Their situation was desperate. A large proportion of their men had been transported by the Doge to the island of St Nicholas, close to Venice, where they could only be supplied with food by boat – and only at the Doge's convenience. They were trapped. As Dandolo remarked, 'I have done everything I could to furnish all that you asked for your Crusade – for a year and a half or more. My people have already lost a great deal. We are all determined you shall pay us what you owe. If you don't, then let me tell you that you shall not move a foot from the island until we have been paid.'

The expedition was launched in October 1202. Even so there were some dissentients, men who left the Crusading army rather than break their vows. Within a fortnight, the city of Zara had fallen to the combined arms of the Crusaders and the Venetians. The Pope was horrified, and all who had taken part were excommunicated. But by now they were so committed that even this ultimate sanction of the Church could

Santa Sophia's minarets and buttresses date from the Turkish conquest of 1453.

not turn them back. Unfortunately the riches anticipated in the capture and loot of Zara fell far short of expectations. The Crusaders now found themselves in a ruined town, in a hostile country, and in the midst of winter.

Doge Dandolo, we learn, 'seeing that they were disturbed by their predicament', called a meeting and addressed them. 'My Lords,' he said, 'there is in Greece a country that is rich and well supplied with everything you need. If we could only find a reasonable excuse to go there and take what we want to see us on our way . . . we could easily manage to get ourselves to the lands overseas.' The Marquis of Montferrat, who was clearly in the plot, rose to his feet and said that he had recently met the true heir to the throne of Constantinople, the young Alexius. 'If we take him with us, we can justifiably enter the territory of Constantinople, and secure our stores and provisions, for he is the legitimate Emperor.' All was now set for the invasion of the Byzantine Empire and for an attack on Constantinople, if its Emperor and its people were not prepared to treat with the army of the Fourth Crusade and the navy of Venice.

On the morning of 5 July, 1203, the galleys of the Venetians preceded the main body of the fleet across the narrow waters from the Asiatic coast opposite Constantinople and dropped anchor off the suburb of Galata on the northern side of the Golden Horn. The Byzantines watched them in trepidation. Gone were the days when theirs was the mightiest fleet in the eastern Mediterranean. A succession of weak Emperors and corrupt administrators had reduced Constantinople's first line of defence to a shadow. They had reluctantly grown used over the years to the passage of Crusaders through their realms; they had dealt with them, traded and bartered with them – and had always been highly delighted to see these 'barbarous Franks' heading eastward against the Moslems. But now it looked very much as if they were intending to bring their arms against the walls of the 'God-guarded City' itself. 'When the people of the city saw the great fleet and army, and heard the sound of the drums and trumpets, making a tremendous noise, all of them without exception armed thenselves and stood on the roofs of their houses. It must have seemed to them as if the sea and the earth were shaking, and as if all the water was covered with ships. Meanwhile the Emperor had come down with his armed forces to defend the shore . . .'

Unfortunately, as events were later to prove, the morale of the Byzantine army was at a low ebb, the Emperor was mistrusted by many and actively disliked by others, and not only the navy but the very walled defences of the city had in many places fallen into disrepair. At

166

the sight of the Crusaders landing, the nobility on their fine horses which had made the passage in specially-designed transports (Venice thought of everything), the Byzantine army and Alexius III fled the scene. The next move of the invaders was to invest the Tower of Galata, one of the city's strong points on the northern side of the Golden Horn, from which ran a giant chain secured, to the south, at the foot of the city walls. In times of emergency this chain was hauled up by a giant windlass, thus preventing the passage of invading ships into the harbour of the Horn. Despite an attack by the Greeks on the army's beach-head, the result was a foregone conclusion. The all-important tower fell to the Crusaders, who killed most of the defenders. At the same time the Venetians – those masters of all things nautical – were dismantling the windlass and unshackling the great cable. The harbour was now open. The galleys of Venice swept in, to encounter but little opposition from the sad remnants of the imperial fleet that lay within. By the morning of the following day the whole of the Venetian fleet, galleys, transports, and merchantmen, was at anchor inside the Golden Horn.

The Emperor was now informed that the sole object of the expedition was to ensure that the rightful ruler of Constantinople was placed on the throne. If this demand was acceded to, then Alexius III might himself leave in safety and with his personal property. The Emperor, quite rightly, did not trust them and, in any case, who were these Franks to decide who was to rule the ancient and sacred city of Byzantium? The intent of the message, however, was understood by others: remove this false Emperor, install our protégé, pay us and victual us and we will leave you in peace. Since Alexius III was far from popular and since many of

The Conquest of Constantinople : from Villehardouin's chronicle of the Fourth Crusade, La Conquête de Constantinople.

the citizens foresaw ruin if they tried to hold out, inevitably the seed of a party dedicated to the removal of the current Emperor was sown on fertile ground.

The first main event in the campaign took place on 17 July, 1203, when the Venetians and the Crusaders made an attack on the northern walls of Constantinople which faced onto the Golden Horn. Doge Dandolo, blind and old though he was, was aboard the first ship to beach itself below the once-indomitable walls of Constantinople. '. . . He stood in the prow of his galley, while above him waved the banner of St Mark. He cried out to his men to drive on for the shore unless they wished to incur his utmost displeasure. As the galley's bows grounded, he and they leaped out and planted the banner on the shore. As soon as the other Venetians saw that the Doge's galley was the first to touch down, they all dashed forward and beached their ships.' It was a triumph not only of military and naval warfare, but of morale. The Venetians at this period in their history were convinced that no power on earth could beat them at sea, while the Crusaders – although engaged in an infamous enterprise against the greatest bastion of Christendom – were equally convinced that no man could stand up to their swords.

Their initial success was not to last, largely due to the fighting abilities of the Emperor's bodyguard, the Warings or Varingian Guard. This was a *corps d'élite* largely formed of Danes and Swedes, as well as English descended from those who had left their homeland after its conquest by William of Normandy. Armed with battle-axes, they were stronger and taller than the average man, and they wreaked havoc among the Venetians and other Latins who had got upon the walls or into the city. It was largely due to their intervention that Constantinople did not fall at this first assault. In southern Italy, Sicily, on the Adriatic coastline, the Warings had fought the Byzantines' battles for over a century, being engaged against the advancing power of the Normans in the West and the Turks in the East. 'They retained their sturdy northern independence in the midst of a corrupt court . . .' And the court was certainly corrupt. Within twenty-four hours of this first attack upon the walls, the Emperor Alexius III, aware of the plots against him as well, possibly, as his inability to charge the Byzantines with any enthusiasm for his

Opposite: *St Louis leaves Paris on the Seventh Crusade in 1248: from an early fourteenth-century French manuscript.*

Overleaf: *The Crusades of St Louis: a map of the country surrounding the Mediterranean: from an early fifteenth-century manuscript.*

konstantinople
ermenie
sime
iherusalem
eypre
egypte
acre
damiete
maldoire
babiloinne
flum
denile

cause, had fled the city. The blinded ex-Emperor, the father of the young Alexius, whom the Venetians and the Crusaders were proposing, was led up from the dungeons and reinstated on the throne.

This was a severe blow to the leaders of the Fourth Crusade. They had imagined that Isaac was dead. The Byzantines had forestalled them. If the father was still alive, then the son's claims were null and void. However, it did not take long to find a way round this apparent obstacle. Father and son were reunited, Alexius promising to place the whole Empire under the spiritual jurisdiction of Rome – something, the ex-communicated Crusaders felt, that must surely restore their favour with the Pope. Alexius also made many other promises, the loan of a fleet to take them against the Moslems, a large sum in silver and a year's provisions, as well as 10,000 men of his own who would join the Crusade. He could fulfil none of these promises. The Treasury was drained, the Empire was bled dry, and father and son were compelled to prevaricate. The Venetians and Crusaders meanwhile withdrew from the city, made camp on the northern side of the Horn, and lay there a shadowy menace which the Byzantines could not help but see every day of their lives.

It was, as so often in Constantinople, a harsh autumn and winter. But the particular harshness on this occasion was due not only to the snow-laden winds from Russia, but to the sight of the Crusaders and their allies swaggering through the streets of their city, despising them for their apparently supine attitude, and showing all the arrogance of men who knew that they could, if provoked, take Constantinople without very much trouble. It was inevitable that there should be brawls between the citizens and these foreigners, almost inevitable equally that, in a city built largely of wood, undisciplined soldiery should cause riots in which the fire-risk was forgotten. Indignant at finding that the Byzantines had been so tolerant as to permit Moslems – and even a mosque – within the walls, they attacked the Saracen quarter and the mosque, the Greeks endeavouring to protect these guests within their walls. Somehow or other in the affray a fire broke out – 'the greatest' says the contemporary Greek historian Nicetas, 'that had ever occurred in the city.' The wind was strong from the north, and the flames leaped throughout Constantinople, destroying one of the richest parts of the city and running as far as the Hippodrome and Santa Sophia itself. Only the stone and marble construction of these great buildings saved them from the holocaust. 'The Crusaders', as Villehardouin, one of the leaders of

Opposite: *The coffin of St Louis is carried on board ship in Tunis: from* Les Grandes Chroniques de France, *c.1460.*

the expedition, tells us, 'were overwhelmed with grief as they watched great churches and palaces being burnt to the ground. The broad streets where the merchants lived were engulfed in the inferno.' The fire lasted eight days and cut a swathe over three miles wide through the heart of Constantinople – an area bigger perhaps than any other contemporary city in Europe. But still the giant survived.

The young Alexius during this time had been away with a company of the Crusaders, endeavouring to get all the cities in the neighbourhood to accept him as Emperor. When he returned, it was to find that neither he nor his father was popular with the people, and that there was another aspirant to the throne. This was Alexius Ducas, a son-in-law of the self-exiled late Emperor, and known to the people as Murtzuphulus, 'The bushy-eyebrowed'. A man of fire and character, he was determined to seize power and put some spirit into the people. In the meantime, Alexius and his father Isaac were in growing disfavour with Venetians and Crusaders alike, owing to their inability to carry out the terms to which they had agreed. Short of ships, short of soldiers, and – even more important as far as the invaders were concerned – short

The Nave of Santa Sophia, Constantinople.

of cash, they could not prevaricate for ever. After a last formal demand for the Byzantines to fulfil their promises, 'Open warfare now began, each side doing its best to inflict damage upon the other, both by land and by sea.'

An attempt by the Byzantines on 1 January, 1204 to destroy the Venetian fleet by fireships met with complete failure and, though 'the flames from them rose so high that the very sea seemed to be on fire', the competent sailors of the Republic managed to stave them off from doing any real damage and propelled them out beyond the Golden Horn where the swift-running current of the Bosporus soon whirled them away to the south of Constantinople. This attack was seen as the doing of their former protégé Alexius, and from now on the invaders would have no truck with him. It was the moment for Murtzuphulus to strike, and he found the populace at his back. The cry went up 'Away with Alexius and his father!' Murtzuphulus, having deceived the Waring Guard – who remained faithful to the Emperor – as to his whereabouts, seized Alexius, that pawn in the hands of Philip of Swabia and the Crusaders, stripped him of his imperial insignia (which he promptly donned himself) and had the youth imprisoned. His father in the meantime had conveniently died – or possibly been assisted in his departure from the world. Not very long afterwards, Murtzuphulus, aware of the fact that imprisoned claimants to the throne had a way of exciting pity or even, as Alexius had already done, of escaping, had him strangled. The Crusaders' last claim to have any authority or rights to the control of Constantinople and the Empire vanished with him.

A man of action, Murtzuphulus did all he could to put the city into a state of readiness for the siege which he knew must come. He was faced with the inertia that had overcome the Byzantines during the recent period of their history. He was faced also with the desire on the part of many officials and merchants to come to terms with this dangerous enemy. Yield to the Venetians and Crusaders, was the opinion of many – and then we can tame them and use them for our own purpose against the Turk. On the other hand, it was clear to the besiegers that they had no option but to comply with the will of Venice and storm the city. They needed the money to pay their debts, and without the Venetian fleet there was no possibility of their escaping from this hostile shore and fulfilling the purpose for which they had originally set out. On Friday morning, 9 April, 1204, the great attack was launched. Scaling bridges were erected on the galleys' bows to permit the men to land on the top of Constantinople's formidable walls. Rock- and spear-hurling catapults opened fire from the transports upon the defenders who, despite the efforts that Murtzuphulus had made to strengthen their positions, were soon overwhelmed by the efficiency as well as the violence of the assault. Nevertheless, it was not until 13 April, that the combined forces of the Crusaders and the Venetians had securely established themselves within the walls. They now proceeded to take possession of what was then the greatest city in the world. Constantinople lay almost defenceless before a blood-mad army which, disregarding any of the ideals with which it was supposed to have set out, proceeded to behave like the barbarians they were. Even the shameful carnage of massacre in Jerusalem at the close of the First Crusade was eclipsed by these successors. In the horrified words of Villehardouin, who actually witnessed the scene: 'The army spread through the city and began to loot it . . . They seized gold and silver, precious stones and tableware of precious metals, silks and satins, coats of fur – squirrel, ermine and miniver – and indeed all the riches of the earth. I stake my word that never had any army gained so much plunder in the whole history of the world . . .'

It was the betrayal by the Western Church of all the principles it theoretically stood for, and it was to end in a permanent schism between the Orthodox Church and the Church of Rome which far exceeded the division that had existed before. As Nicetas put it: 'They had taken up the Cross and had sworn on it and on the Holy Gospels that they would pass over the lands of Christians without shedding blood . . . They had promised to keep themselves chaste while they bore the Cross as befitted the soldiers of Christ. But instead of defending his tomb, they had outraged the faithful who are members of Him. They used Christians worse than the Arabs, for at least the Arabs respected women . . . They respected nothing, neither the churches, nor the sacred images of Christ and his Saints! They acted like enemies of the Cross! They committed atrocities upon men, respectable women, virgins, and young girls!'

Monasteries and convents were sacked, the sacred precincts of Santa Sophia were invaded by drunken hordes, while whores danced before the altar and the soldiery despoiled the cathedral of the accumulated wealth of centuries. The Venetians, anxious to embellish their own city, were foremost among the looters. Among the innumerable works of art that went back to the City of the Lagoons were the bronze horses that now stand over the entrance to St Mark's. Magnificent bronzes from the ancient world, such as the famous Hercules of Lysippus, a colossal Hera from the island of Samos, a group representing Augustus celebrating his victory over Antony and Cleopatra – all these and dozens like them were hurled away to the smelting furnaces. A statue of Helen of Troy which Nicetas described as 'fairer than the evening air, clad in the beauty of a thousand stars' was dragged away to be broken up. If such was the treatment accorded to the city's fabulous treasures it cannot be expected that the Byzantines themselves had anything to hope for. 'On all sides there was nothing to be heard but cries, groans, laments and screams. Here there were fights and quarrels over loot, there prisoners were being led away, and everywhere among the raped and wounded lay the dead.'

Murtzuphulus had fled in company with thousands of the city's inhabitants. Constantinople, the Byzantine Empire, the culture and tradition of centuries, the arm which had held at bay the enemies of Christendom ever since its foundation, was no more. In their place the Crusaders were to erect a ramshackle series of principalities and minor states as primitive in their feudal conception as the Empire, from whose body they carved their petty pieces, had been grand and noble. After only fifty-seven years, the Palaeologus family who had established themselves in Nicaea in Asia Minor managed to return and evict the Latins. For two further centuries they and their successors contrived to hold together the remnants of the Empire. The end was inevitable. In 1453 the conquering forces of Mehmet II, Sultan of the Ottomans, swept into the city and within a few years had turned it into the capital of the Turkish Empire. The Turks behaved far better than the Venetians and Crusaders had done. Little in history can exceed the monstrous crimes of the soldiers and sailors of the Fourth Crusade. To all intents and purposes they irrevocably destroyed the Crusading Movement. Far worse than that, they let the Ottoman Turk into Europe. Their descendants would long regret the day when Constantinople fell to the Venetians and the soldiers of the Fourth Crusade.

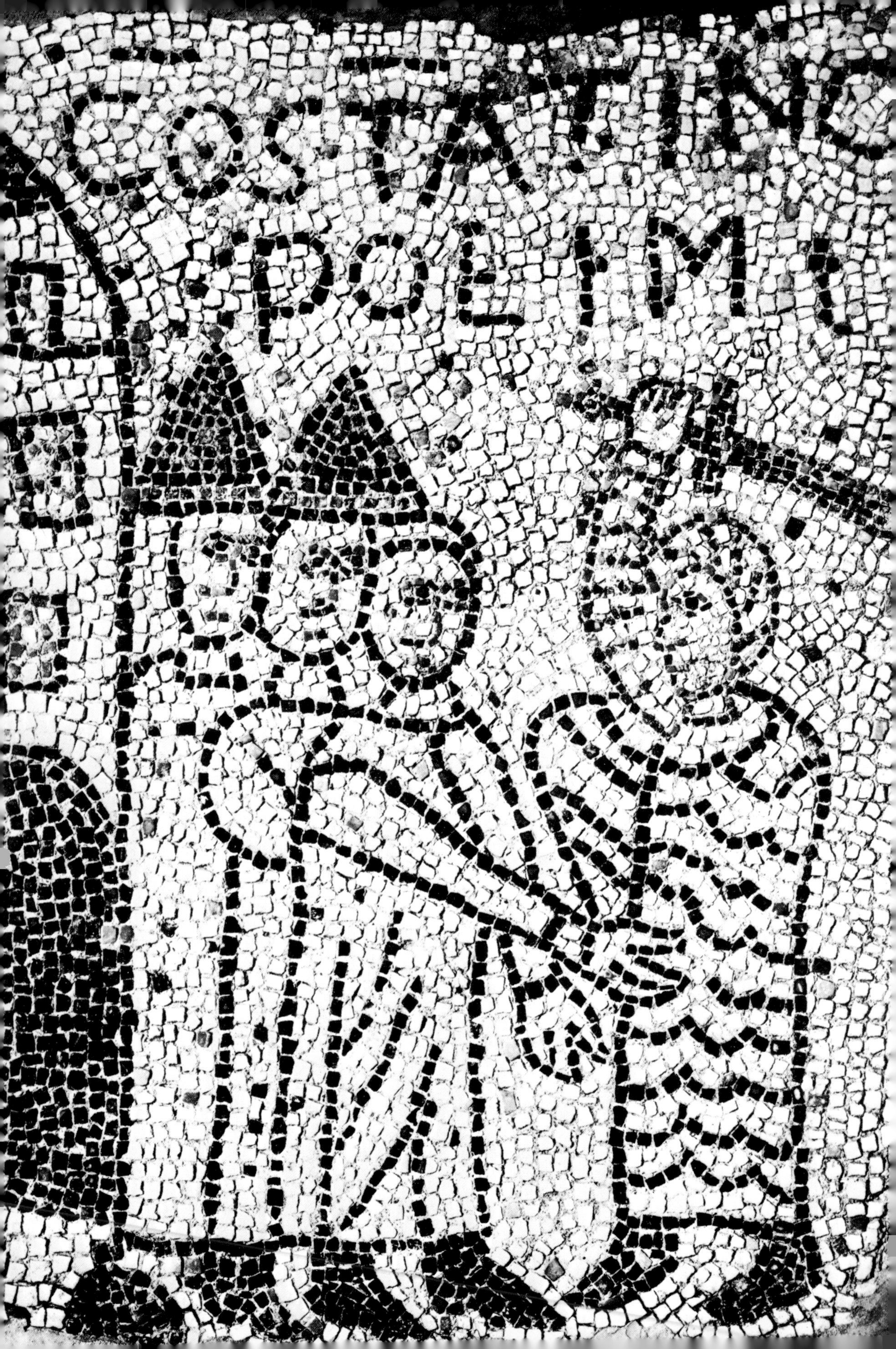

The Children's Crusade

The diversion of the Fourth Crusade to Constantinople, disastrous though it was for the Byzantines, their empire, and for Europe, was not without some indirect benefit to the small Latin kingdom that Richard Coeur-de-Lion had managed to consolidate. For one thing, a truce between King Amalric II and Sultan Al-Adil, Saladin's brother and successor, gave the Latins a chance to rebuild their cities and fortifications, and to conduct their trading in peace. While Al-Adil was himself kept busy in maintaining his own inheritance he was quite willing to leave the Christians in peace, for he had no wish to provoke a further Crusade. After the death of Amalric in 1205 the kingdom was governed by a wise old knight, Jean of Ibelin, who held it in trust for its future Queen, the thirteen-year-old Marie. When she reached eighteen it was necessary to find a husband for her and a deputation was sent to France for this purpose. They hoped no doubt to bring back a rich and powerful nobleman who would make a strong king and who would initiate the recovery of Jerusalem. Unfortunately the only candidate for Marie's hand was John of Brienne, who brought neither money nor prestige to the throne, let alone youth, for he was sixty. He was, however, luckily for the Latins, a man who had matured in the ways of the world and diplomacy. He was unlikely to be rash and hot-headed, and he very soon enjoyed the respect of his subjects and of the powerful Military Orders. He was not averse to allowing the latter to try their arm against the enemy in Egypt, but an unsuccessful expedition against Damietta which lasted for three years finally convinced both John of Brienne and the Military Orders that they were not yet strong enough to achieve any success against Egypt, which was the hard core of their enemies. In 1218,

Opposite: *Mosaic floor in the Church of S Giovanni in Ravenna, representing the Fall of Constantinople.*

while operations against Damietta were still proceeding, Al-Adil died in Damascus. A worthy successor to Saladin, he had held his empire together for eighteen years, and had proved himself tolerant and states-manlike in his dealings with the Latins.

Far away in Europe, during these years while the remaining posses-sions in *Outremer* were enjoying a revival of prosperity, there had been other and very strange attempts to rouse once more the Crusading spirit and to send an army to recapture Jerusalem. It is evidence perhaps of the decline among the more educated adults of that unquestioning belief which had motivated, for instance, the People's Crusade that 'the spark from Heaven' now fell among children. In May 1212 a peasant boy called Stephen was brought before King Philip of France at his court at Saint-Denis. The boy asserted that he had had a vision of Christ and that he had been told to go out into the world to preach a Crusade to recover the Holy Places. Philip, who had a great many other things on his mind, not unnaturally dismissed young Stephen with the sage advice that he should go back to his home and attend to his duties: he was a shepherd. The boy had almost certainly derived the idea of his myster-ious visitor from one or more of the many itinerant preachers who were still active throughout France and other parts of western Europe, calling on people to repent and recapture Jerusalem. Undaunted by the royal rebuff, Stephen proceeded to preach the Crusade from Saint-Denis itself throughout large parts of France, while other young converts took the word back to their home districts.

Astonishing as it may seem to an inhabitant of the twentieth century, within a month thousands of children, a few of noble birth, as well as some clerics and other devout adults had followed the oriflamme of St Denis. This was a pointed banner of red silk which it had been the custom of the kings of France to receive from the abbot of Saint-Denis whenever they set out for battle. It had been adopted by young Stephen and his followers as the token of their resolve to recapture the Holy City. By the time that they reached Marseilles in the high summer of 1212 many of the children had either given up in despair, or died by the way-side. Nevertheless it was a large gathering, numbering many thousands, who finally poured into the ancient city. They believed implicitly, as Stephen had told them, that the waters of the Mediterranean would part and that with God's grace they would walk dryshod across to Palestine. Their disillusionment at the non-fulfilment of this miracle caused many of them to turn back to seek their homes. Even so, a large number, including some pilgrims and priests, still waited at the water-side con-vinced that in due course the miracle would happen.

Pope Innocent III, 1198-1216 : from a mosaic, c.1200.

Far more prosaic, and on the surface of it natural enough, was the arrival of two Marseilles merchants who offered to carry them across the sea. This, they said, they would do without payment, and for the greater glory of God. A small armada of seven ships put out to sea. Two of them were wrecked on an island south of Sardinia with the loss of all aboard, while the other five—as arranged by the kindly Marseillais merchants, whose names, we learn, were Iron Hugh and Pig William— met up by arrangement with slavers from the Barbary Coast. The survivors of the Children's Crusade were sold in the great slave market at Bougie, many of them finally ending up in Alexandria. One of the adults, a young priest, returned years later to France and told of the tragic end of this most inconsequential and pathetic of all Crusades. Faith, as had been shown on previous occasions, would neither move mountains nor part seas.

The news of Stephen's preaching reached Germany within a few weeks of his departure from Saint-Denis and a German youth, Nicholas, not to be outdone by the French embarked on a similar preaching mission. He collected behind him a horde of children who streamed out from German cities and villages, determined to prove that they could succeed – where the adults had failed – in capturing the Holy Land. Had not The Master himself said: 'Suffer the little children to come unto me, for of such is the Kingdom of Heaven'? The whole extraordinary episode possibly gave rise to the legend of the Pied Piper of Hamelin.

In both of these streams that fed the river of the Children's Crusade of 1212 it must be seen that the children did not always leave their homes to parental tears and rejecting the warmth and security of the family hearth. Quite often, in the conditions obtaining among the European peasantry at that time, the parents can only have been relieved of the burden of some useless mouths. Life was very hard in northern Europe. If that dream of a land flowing with milk and honey which had seduced their ancestors in 1096 now exercised its siren spell over their children there were many parents who could only wish them well. Since, whatever some of the more sophisticated among the nations might think, the imminence of the Second Coming was still widely believed in by those who had little other cause for hope, the possibility that their children might find a salvation not to be found in town garret or peasant cottage was not to be despised. Both boys and girls to the number of twenty thousand followed the piper. Some of them crossed the Alps by the Mont Cenis pass and others by Saint Gotthard into Italy. The first arrived at Genoa. Again the waters obstinately refused to open before them. Many stayed to become adopted Genoese citizens, others under Nicholas himself went on to Pisa and Rome. The Pope, Innocent III, profound believer in the Crusading movement though he was (and well disillusioned, one might have thought, by the Fourth Crusade) was not sufficiently cynical to permit these ignorant children to perform their vows. He suggested that they all returned to their homes and carried out their Crusading dreams when they were grown up. Even so, at least two shiploads of German children are said to have embarked at Pisa, never to be heard of again.

The moral implications of the Children's Crusades did not go unremarked by the Pope: 'The very children put us to shame,' he wrote, 'for while we sleep they go forth gladly to conquer the Holy Land.' In 1215, at the fourth Lateran Council, he proclaimed a Crusade for all Europe, designed to take place in 1217. A year before the first Crusaders disembarked at Acre, Pope Innocent III died in Perugia. He had endeavoured to revive the Crusading spirit in Europe and is often considered one of the greatest of the Popes. Yet the only successful Crusade that occurred during his pontificate was the one that destroyed Byzantium and its empire. Another 'success', if it could be called such, was his initiation of the Crusade against the Albigensian heretics which was to end in the complete extinction of the brilliant Provençal culture of southern France. It is not without significance that the Fifth Crusade which he had initiated was to be more remarkable for the division of the command between the papal legate, Cardinal Pelagius, and the King of Jerusalem, John of Brienne, than for anything else.

Crusader Hugh of Vaudemont returns to his wife: twelfth-century stone carving.

le grit a petit pint.
Or disons dont q̃
quant grace nous
fist dieu le tout puissai
quant il nous deffen
Ci deuise comment da
miete fu prinse.

nuer la ou nous attia
mes a pie et coumnes
sus a nos ennemis q̃
qui estoient a cheual.

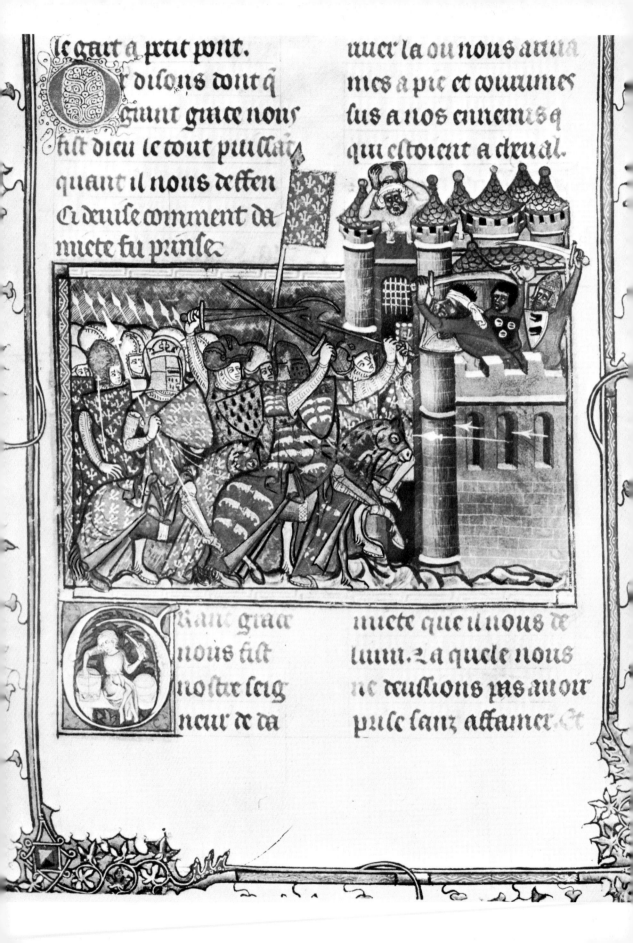

Grant grace
nous fist
nostre seig
neur de da

miete que il nous de
liurai. La quele nous
ne deuisions pas auoir
prise sanz affamer. Et

Failure in Egypt

John of Brienne, who had been conducting the operations against Damietta for over three months, was far from pleased when, in September 1218, Cardinal Pelagius, the papal legate appointed by Pope Innocent, arrived on the scene. The latter claimed that he was the rightful commander-in-chief of all Christian forces, a position which could not be denied him since, whatever John of Brienne and others may have felt, it was upon the Pope that they were dependent for the recruitment of men, munitions, and money for *Outremer*. These dissensions between the ecclesiastical and the lay motives had been at the root of nearly all the trouble in the Crusades from the very beginning.

The year 1219 opened prosperously for the Franks. Damietta seemed within their grasp and the Sultan Al-Kamil, who had succeeded Al-Adil the year before, was so disturbed when he realised that fresh Crusaders were arriving almost daily and that their intention was clearly to make for Cairo that he decided to be conciliatory. (As time was to prove he was as wise and sensible as his two great predecessors.) Quite apart from the Crusaders he had his own problems with the Seljuk Turks and others who were tearing at the fabric of the empire. Accordingly, he afforded Pelagius and John of Brienne terms which it must have seemed to any reasonable man were more than acceptable. The Kingdom of Jerusalem would be returned to them just as it had been before the battle of Hattin, with the exception of territory east of the Jordan. Even here, he was prepared to pay a tribute for any of the castles that he might retain. He would also return to them that relic which he knew meant so much to the Christians, the True Cross captured at Hattin.

At first sight it seems difficult to believe that such terms were turned down, but Pelagius was a stubborn intransigent Spaniard who had little or no knowledge of the conduct of affairs in the East. Possibly he assumed that the very fact the Sultan was prepared to offer terms meant that he could be pushed to make even further concessions. He may well have thought that Al-Kamil had so many problems on his hands that, if the Crusaders could capture Damietta, all Egypt lay before them. Such a prize could hardly be ignored, for Egypt, one of the wealthiest countries in the world at that time, was the core of Mohammedanism. Capture Egypt, and the whole of the East fell into your hands – such, almost certainly, was the reasoning of the Cardinal.

In the August of 1219 there was a near-mutiny among the infantry. Worn out by their continual irksome conditions under that 'lion sun' which can almost deprive a man of reason they insisted on being allowed to make a concerted attack on the Sultan's camp. The Moslems feigned retreat and then counter-attacked. Pelagius now showed that when it came to battle conditions he was inexperienced. Furthermore, the troops had no confidence in him. Only the resolution and skill of King John,

St Francis preaches to the birds: from Matthew Paris's Historia Major II.

backed by the discipline of the Military Orders, saved a retreat from becoming a headlong rout. Sensing that this was surely a good moment for reopening negotiations, Al-Kamil repeated his offer. Just as promptly

Cardinal Pelagius turned it down. It was he who was now on the defensive, but he must have sensed that the Sultan's willingness to concede the Kingdom of Jerusalem at such a moment meant that, if the Crusaders could achieve a victory, he could obtain all and even more than he had ever hoped for.

There had been one curious spectator during this phase of the siege of Damietta, possibly the only true Christian to be present during any of the Crusades. This was a man who truly believed the words to be found in St Matthew: 'Freely have you received, freely give. Carry neither gold nor silver nor money in your girdles, nor bag, nor two coats, nor sandals, nor staff, for the workman is worthy of his hire.' Francis of Assisi, most lovable of saints (to be canonised within two years of his death), had come East like many another before him to seek inspiration in the Holy Land. In stark contrast to the belligerent political Cardinal was the poor brother who loved all living creatures. 'Blessed be the peacemakers'. Francis asked the Cardinal if he might be permitted to cross over into enemy lines and talk with the Sultan. No harm could come of it, Pelagius thought, and sent him under a flag of truce to the Sultan's encampment. As Sir Steven Runciman puts it: 'The Moslem guards were suspicious at first but soon decided that anyone so simple, so gentle and so dirty must be mad, and treated him with the respect due to a man who had been touched by God.' Francis was taken before Al-Kamil and preached the Gospel to him on several occasions. He is reputed to have said that he would willingly undergo the ordeal by fire if the Sultan and his followers would be converted. The civilized and sophisticated Moslem was quite unwilling to allow this simple man to undergo so barbarous a test. He listened courteously and with interest to the belief held by *il poverello*, did not openly dismiss it, but asked him to pray that he, Al-Kamil, might come to know the true faith. Francis was offered rich gifts, all of which he refused, and was then returned under a guard of honour to the Christian lines. Like many another, then and in later centuries, he had found out that, while it is easy enough to lead a peace-mission into the East, it is more than difficult to achieve any results.

At long last, after a siege that had lasted eighteen months, Damietta fell to the Crusaders. They had been months, both for besiegers and besieged, of almost unendurable hardship: shortage of water and of rations, backbreaking manual work in the trenches, then the rains of winter, and then again the blinding, fly-ridden heat of summer. The Crusades were far from being, as they have so often been portrayed, a series of glamorous campaigns in which mounted knights came thundering to the charge, in which sultans and emirs emerged from silken tents to meet them, and in which romantic heroes met hand-to-hand in single combat. At Damietta as at Acre the reality was not so far removed from trench warfare in the First World War, or the thirst, short commons, sandstorms, and desert sores of the North African campaigns of the Second World War.

Established in Damietta, the Franks with their secure supply lines from the sea behind them, began to feel an optimisim that they had not known for many a year. It seemed that it was only a question of time

The siege of Damietta from the sea;
soldiers assault the city walls:
from Matthew Paris's Historia Major II, *c.1219.*

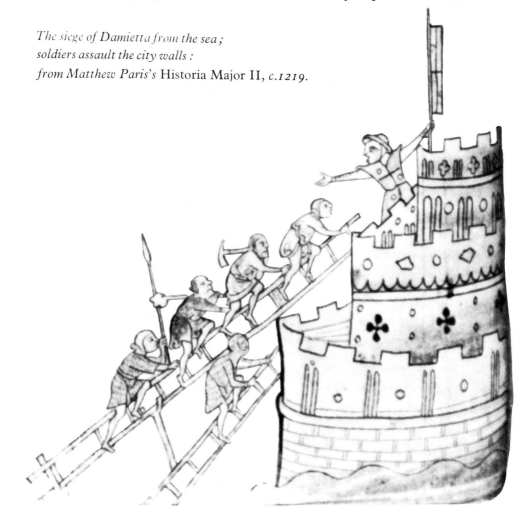

before, with the arrival of fresh reinforcements from Europe, they could storm into Egypt and take Cairo. John of Brienne returned to Acre. He had an Armenian wife and he was laying claim to the throne of that country. In the event, his wife and his small son died and once again the future of the Kingdom of Jerusalem – if they should regain it – was uncertain. Cardinal Pelagius in the meantime proceeded to rule Damietta like a monarch. He saw himself most probably as the future ruler of all Egypt, subject only to the Pope. There seems little doubt that, if the Crusaders had not abandoned themselves in their usual fashion to sacking and looting the city, but had immediately moved on, Cairo would indeed have been theirs.

For over a year the Crusaders waited at Damietta. It was rumoured

that the Emperor Frederick II would soon be on his way with a large army, which would be more than enough to give the Christians the impetus to move successfully into Egypt. But the months went by, and still there was no sign of the Emperor, so at last Pelagius decided to take action on his own account. He summoned John of Brienne back to Damietta and, although the latter did all he could to persuade the Cardinal to wait for Frederick, Pelagius gave the orders to advance. In July 1221, the Crusading army moved southward down the eastern bank of the Nile to Fariskur. Although they left behind a large garrison at Damietta it was still a very formidable force that was advancing into Egypt. Contemporary accounts speak of over 600 ships, 5,000 knights, 40,000 infantrymen and over 4,000 archers. With them also went a vast host of pilgrims and camp-followers. By the end of July they had passed Fariskur and were encamped on a narrow spit of land near Bahr al-Saghir. Al-Kamil reiterated the terms that he had offered them before the fall of Damietta; the return of Jerusalem and the Kingdom, and in addition a thirty-year peace. Once again Pelagius refused.

Little did the Cardinal, or indeed any of the other Crusaders, know that they were in an untenable position. It was the season of the annual rise of the Nile. An army under Al-Kamil's brothers had crossed the river behind them and cut them off from Damietta, while a fleet of his ships had come down into the Nile by a canal to the north of them and thus held the Crusading fleet at its mercy. At this point Al-Kamil ordered the sluices on the eastern bank to be opened, and the Crusaders in their low-lying land found themselves trapped by rising water. Mounted knights, foot-soldiers, and all the supply-train of the army found themselves floundering and slipping in a land that had suddenly become water-logged. The Franks struggled back. There was nothing for it but retreat, and steadily the Nile rose around them. On 28 July, Pelagius sued for peace. The Crusade was at an end, any hopes of invading Egypt were finally extinguished.

Even at this moment Al-Kamil remained generous in his terms. They might evacuate Egypt unmolested, Pelagius, King John, and other notables remaining as hostages until Damietta had been evacuated. At the same time an exchange of prisoners was agreed upon, and a truce between the two parties to last for eight years, only to be broken if a King or an Emperor came to the East. Thousands of men had been lost during the retreat, the Moslem world had had its confidence restored, and once again the Christians from Europe had seen a Crusade that had seemed to promise success expire in dismal failure. It is difficult accurately to apportion the blame, but certainly John of Brienne comes out of the long campaign with considerable credit. Perhaps Sir Ernest Barker best summed up the Fifth Crusade when he wrote: 'If Frederick had only come in person, a single month of his presence might have meant everything: if Pelagius had only listened to King John, the sultan was ready to concede practically everything which was at issue. Unhappily Frederick preferred to put his Sicilian house in order, and the legate preferred to listen to the Italians, who had their own commercial reasons for wishing to establish a strong position in Egypt, and to the Templars and Hospitallers, who did not feel satisfied by the terms offered by the Sultan, because he wished to retain in his hands the two fortresses of Krak and Montreal . . .' Throughout the whole affair Al-Kamil had behaved with exemplary good sense. He had offered what he possibly knew the Crusaders could never hold in the long run – the Kingdom of Jerusalem – and even in the end he made the great concession of returning to them the True Cross.

Oliver of Cologne, one of the leaders of the German contingent among the Crusaders, wrote of that Moslem hospitality which was in such marked contrast to the intolerance of the Christians: 'The people whose sons and daughters, brothers and sisters we had killed, whose substance we had plundered and whom we had driven naked from their homes, now saved us with their food when we were dying of hunger, and assisted us with many kindnesses when we were completely in their power.' It seems a fitting epitaph to the Fifth Crusade, and indeed to practically all these campaigns which the rude West conducted against the civilized East.

Saracens and Christians fight at Damietta: from Historia Major II.

Success at Last

Frederick II, Holy Roman Emperor and King of Sicily, was the grandson of the great Frederick I, 'Barbarossa', whose untimely death had led to the disintegration of the Third Crusade. Born in Italy, Frederick II had been crowned King of Germany in 1215 and crowned Emperor at Rome on 22 November, 1220, at which time he had made lavish promises to the Pope that he would go on Crusade to regain the Holy Land. He had made these promises before, as early as 1215 in fact, but the intervening years had been largely spent in restoring order in his kingdom of Sicily, a land then, as so often in its history, seething with discontent. *Stupor Mundi*, his contemporaries were to call him, the Wonder of the World. By blood half-German, half-Norman, he was at heart wholly Sicilian. And the Sicily where he had been crowned king at Palermo in 1198 was an island where the manners, *mores* and culture – stemming from the island's occupation by Byzantines and then by Arabs – were Greco-Arabic. Machiavelli might well have had him in mind when he wrote *The Prince*, and indeed Frederick II was all and a great deal more than Machiavelli's hero, Cesare Borgia: 'Our experience has been that those princes who have done great things have held good faith of little account, and have known how to circumvent the intellect of men by craft, and in the end have overcome those who have relied upon their word . . . it is necessary to be a great pretender and dissembler; and men are so simple and so subject to present necessities that he who seeks to deceive will always find someone who will allow himself to be deceived.'

Fluent in six languages, French, German, Italian, Latin, Greek, and Arabic, Frederick was the first intellectual of any consequence to involve himself in the affairs of *Outremer*, a land which curiously enough

Opposite: *Battle scene in the civil war between Palestine and Cyprus: from the* Maciejowski Bible, *early thirteenth-century.*

he never understood and seems to have actively disliked. The fact was that the concepts of people like the Templars and Hospitallers were medieval, while Frederick was a forerunner of the Renaissance; *homo universalis* if ever there was one. A patron of the arts, a mathematician, philosopher, a writer at whose court, as Dante points out, Italian poetry had its birth, Frederick could have little in common with rough Crusaders and ascetic (theoretically at any rate) military orders. He temporised as long as he could about fulfilling his promise to the Pope to take the Cross and it was not until the failure of the Fifth Crusade that he could be forced to make any move. The Pope, Honorius III, had cannily tried to bind him to the Holy Land by arranging a marriage with the daughter of John of Brienne, Isabella. Since the right to the throne of Jerusalem passed through the female line, this automatically made Frederick King of Jerusalem, thus dispossessing John of Brienne who had – at least so Frederick reasoned – only held the title by courtesy of the kingdom until such time as his daughter should be grown up and married. This was the strange Crusader who was to succeed where others had failed, a Crusader to whom was widely attributed the remark that 'Moses, Christ, and Mahomet were all impostors'.

The marriage of Frederick II to Isabella.

Frederick married Isabella in 1225 in the Cathedral at Brindisi, informing John of Brienne at the same time that he was dispossessed, and sending his young wife to the harem that he kept in oriental style at Palermo. Three years later she died after giving birth to a son; a tragic little figure Isabella, not yet seventeen at the time of her death. *Stupor Mundi* still tarried at Brindisi until, in 1227, he felt that he could prevaricate no longer and, having gathered together an army that was mainly German and Italian, he set sail for Palestine. On the way, as was common enough among medieval armies where hygiene was scarcely known, 'pestilence' broke out among the troops and Frederick himself fell ill of a fever. Being sensible enough – unlike many other Crusaders – to realise that it was pointless to arrive with shiploads of sick soldiers, he ordered the fleet to turn about and make for Otranto. A new Pope, Gregory IX, now held the keys of the kingdom. He had watched from the sidelines, as it were, the interminable excuses made by this emperor to avoid fulfilling his mission and he came to the conclusion that only the harshest of all edicts would bring Frederick to his senses – and to the understanding that the Pope, and the Pope alone, was the supreme lord of all Christendom. Frederick was excommunicated.

It was not until the summer of 1228 that the Emperor, having sent most of his forces ahead of him, finally embarked for the Crusade. It was an astonishing situation, for no sooner had he set sail than papal troops began invading his Italian territories, while he himself was going to the Holy Land as an excommunicated Crusader. After calling in at Cyprus, where he made sure that all the Cypriots swore allegiance to him as their overlord, he went on to Acre. His reception by the knights and nobles, but above all by the Military Orders of the Templars and Hospitallers, was never a favourable one. Frederick lay under the interdict of excommunication which meant that no one was bound to serve him in any way – the reverse rather, for an excommunicate should be forced to his knees to beg forgiveness. Had it not been for his own troops, never more than a few thousand, and the friendship of the Grand Master of the Teutonic Order (which secured their obedience to him) Frederick could have done little or nothing. As it was, his Crusade, as he rightly saw, was one that must be achieved by diplomacy rather than by arms.

He was fortunate in the fact that Al-Kamil was bedevilled by a great split in the Moslem camp, occasioned mainly by the fact that one of the Ayyubite brothers who between them ruled Syria, Jezireh, and Egypt, had died and the struggle was on for the division of his lands. (Al-Kamil had even sent an emir to Frederick's court in Palermo in 1226 asking the

Emperor to lend assistance to his cause.) Excommunicate, asked in to help one of the enemy, and fully conversant with affairs in the Moslem world, Frederick was in an excellent position for manoeuvring on the political chessboard. In almost all other respects he was at a great disadvantage. Many of the prominent figures in *Outremer*, disliking in any case this half-German king and emperor, were not above being outright insulting.

Frederick, who had been in communication with Al-Kamil, decided that a show of force was at least indicated and marched south from Acre to Jaffa, which he re-fortified, and a winter of hard bargaining began. The Emperor's Greco-Moslem Sicilian training in the ways of the East served him in good stead. He knew just how far to go, when to retract, when to appear to retract, and when to make a concession. Between November 1228 and February of the following year he achieved what many swords and many siege engines had failed to do. He concluded with Al-Kamil the treaty which had eluded John of Brienne, and which had been spurned by Cardinal Pelagius. There was to be a ten-year truce between Christian and Moslem. Jerusalem was to be restored to the Franks, but the Dome of the Rock and the mosque Al-Aqsa were to stay in Moslem hands, while any Moslem might freely enter the city to go to his places of worship. Nazareth and Bethlehem were also handed

Pope Gregory IX, 1227-41.

196

back to the Christians, as well as a narrow strip of land that connected Jerusalem with the port of Acre. The Moslem districts around Sidon, at one time shared between both parties, were to come under Latin control and at the same time there was to be a general exchange of prisoners of war. It was a triumph of diplomacy, and no unnecessary battles had been fought either under the desert sun or in the harsh rains of winter.

Nevertheless it remained highly unpopular on both sides. The Military Orders felt that they had received less than they had been offered in the days when they were at Damietta, the Latin knights and other settlers felt that the corridor between Jerusalem and Acre was indefensible, and the Moslems were incensed at the return to the infidel of the holy city over which they had spilled so much blood. Both Frederick and Al-Kamil were highly unpopular with their co-religionists, the Patriarch of Jerusalem placing an interdict on the city should the Emperor ever enter it, while the imams at Damascus and in Egypt ordered public mourning for the betrayal of Islam.

Frederick was cynical. He knew what power was all about, and he had felt no worse a man since the Pope had deprived him of the sacraments and declared him an outcast. He was determined all the same to add the crown of Jerusalem to his many other worldly titles, for he rightly felt that he had earned it. He had achieved solely by diplomatic bargaining everything that Richard Coeur-de-Lion had so nearly achieved by similar methods, but also with the aid of the sword. The successors of Saladin and of Richard worked, it is true, in a very different climate of opinion but they had managed to bring about an agreed tolerance between Christian and Moslem of which both their predecessors would have approved. Whatever the Templars, the Hospitallers, and others might say, Frederick was now about to enter his capital as its rightful

The capture of the anti-imperial prelates by the Pisans in 1241 : from Matthew Paris's Historia Major II, *c.1255.*

king—even though that was something that they disputed. On 17 March, 1229, accompanied by his Germans and Italians as well as by the Teutonic Knights, the Emperor rode into a Jerusalem that seemed to be empty of Moslem and Christian alike. No local priest would officiate at the ceremony of coronation, nor even at the Mass which must necessarily precede it. Undismayed, Frederick had the crown laid on the altar of Calvary in the Holy Sepulchre and—as Napoleon was to do centuries later at Notre Dame—took it and placed it on his own head. Among those who were present on the occasion, approving of it, were two Englishmen, Peter of Winchester and William of Exeter. Already, so long before the Reformation, the English were beginning to feel that the papal hand was over-heavy and largely governed by material considerations.

Frederick spent no more than a month in the realm whose king he now was. There were troubles and dissensions, open hostility from the Templars among others, and in any case affairs at home necessitated his return to Italy. John of Brienne at the head of the papal forces had invaded his territories, and these were of far more importance to him than this curious hotchpotch of *Outremer*, or even the gracious island of

A retreating army : from the Majiekowski Bible, *early thirteenth-century.*

Cyprus. After forty years of struggle on the part of Crusaders for the recapture of Jerusalem he had restored it to Christendom without a battle or even a blow. It was this perhaps which the Military Orders resented so much. They were brought up to believe in their sword-arm and in the necessity of wading through blood for the restoration of the Kingdom. As for treaties and reading and writing, why they had clerics and secretaries to do that for them. Then along came this red-faced, short-sighted, clean-shaven man (both they and the Arabs considered a beard a sign of masculinity), and by cheating and dealing and bartering like some huckster in a market had seemingly pocketed Jerusalem and the title of king. It was intolerable.

The fact remains that the Sixth Crusade was a success, even if an unpopular one with both Christian and Moslem. Not without a sigh of relief Frederick turned his back on the Holy Land. 'If God had known about Sicily, Christ would have been born there!' He left for Italy in May 1229, overcame the papal armies without too much difficulty, and received absolution from a somewhat chastened Pope Gregory, who was reluctantly forced to admit that this free-thinking sensualist (Frederick's sexual habits were said to be very erratic) had managed to restore Jerusalem into Christian hands where so many others of so much better repute had failed. The Kingdom of Jerusalem as it existed after Frederick's intervention was to last a further fifteen years, the last time that the holy places of Christendom were to be held by Europeans until the twentieth century. They were not happy years, however, for no sooner was the Emperor away than civil war broke out both in Palestine and in Cyprus. It was every man for himself, baron against baron, Templars against Hospitallers, one city against another. The only reason that the Moslems did not capture everything and sweep the Franks into the sea was that they too were divided one against another, and that they had the Mongols and the Tatars on their northern frontiers.

Dissensions

The fifteen years during which the Kingdom of Jerusalem was nominally restored – nominally, for the Moslems could have taken it almost any time they wanted – present a tapestry of anarchy. In 1230, Frederick having become temporarily reconciled with Pope Gregory IX, decided to send an army into the East to sort out his affairs in that area. John of Ibelin, Lord of Beirut, had already overthrown the commission of five barons which the Emperor had left behind to administer the affairs of Cyprus, and was in effect, in the absence of Frederick, the uncrowned king both of Cyprus and Jerusalem. Frederick's legate, Marshal Filanghieri, was to all intents and purposes sent East not to wage war against the Moslems but to restore order among the Christians and secure the Emperor's property.

The barons in Cyprus and *Outremer*, for their part, maintained that as an absentee overlord Frederick had no claim upon them or upon the kingdom. John of Ibelin, who had heard of the approach of Frederick's forces while he was at Acre, guessed rightly that they would make first for Cyprus so, leaving a garrison force behind him, he sailed at once for the island. Meanwhile a gild was formed at Acre which, though nominally religious, represented in fact the political opposition to Frederick II's claims to the territories in the East. By 1233 the Emperor had lost his hold on Cyprus and little remained to him in *Outremer* except the city and seaport of Tyre. Ten years later even Tyre had fallen to the barons, largely led by the great family of Ibelin, and it was they and not Frederick who now controlled Jerusalem. Amid all these feuds and dissensions, preoccupied with their rights and privileges and the control of their various small kingdoms and principalities, the Franks in the East

Opposite: *Crusaders besiege the seaport of Tyre by land and sea: from a fourteenth-century French manuscript.*

had laid themselves open to the vast tidal wave that was soon to engulf
their petty sand-castle defences. Tatars and Khwarismian Turks
swarmed to the north on the boundaries of all Asia, while Egypt under
the command of a brilliant general and a sultan of explosive power and
personality was soon to rise up against them from the south.

In the summer of 1244, 10,000 Khwarismian horsemen swept down
into the territory around Damascus and, finding the city too strong for
them, moved into Galilee. Too late the Grand Masters of the Templars
and the Hospitallers and the Patriarch of Jerusalem realised the danger
to the city. Too late they attempted to restore the defences and reinforce
the garrison. On 11 July the horsemen from the steppes poured into
that ever-beleaguered City of God, plundering and looting, bursting
into the Church of the Holy Sepulchre, killing some 7,000 of the male
inhabitants and enslaving the women and children. Jerusalem was lost
to the Franks for ever, not to come under a European control again
until the twentieth century. What remained of the inhabitants and the
garrison was saved by a Moslem ally who sent troops into the city,
instilled some discipline among the Khwarismians, and ensured the
departure of the Christian survivors on the road to Jaffa. The Khwarismians, for their part, now moved on and joined up with the army of the
Sultan of Egypt, which was under the command of a young Mameluke-

Louis IX with the True Cross and the Crown of Thorns: from Historia Major II.

mir, Rukh ad-Din Baybers. He was destined to become one of the greatest names in the East and to unite the Moslems as no one before, except Saladin, had been able to do.

The Egyptian army was drawn up before Gaza while the Franks with their allies the Moslems of Syria (their leader was the uncle of the Egyptian Sultan, whose kingdom he coveted) came down to meet them. The Syrians were intent on destroying the power of Egypt, while the Christians hoped that in the ensuing conflict they would destroy the Khwarismian menace and once again secure Jerusalem. Thus one sees the extraordinary reversal that has happened in Crusading ideals – Christians allied with Moslems against a common enemy. In the ensuing battle, one which was largely provoked, as had happened on other occasions, by the impetuous belligerence of the Templars, the Syrians were soundly defeated by the Khwarismian horsemen while the Latins who were engaged against the Egyptian army were encircled and finally cut to pieces. Next to the battle of Hattin it was the greatest disaster to befall Crusading arms in the East. The Military Orders were almost completely destroyed, 36 Templars surviving out of over 300, 26 Hospitallers out of an almost similar number, while the Teutonic Order had only three survivors. A contingent of knights from Cyprus was annihilated.

The Mamelukes: from A Voyage to the Holy Land, *1486.*

The victorious Sultan proceeded to move on and take Damascus, establishing an empire that ran from Egypt to the land beyond the Euphrates. On his way north he had tried the defences of Ascalon, which was garrisoned by the Hospitallers, but had found them too strong and had wisely moved on. He reckoned that the great fortress-port would fall to him in due course either by a sea blockade or by a combination of this and a frontal assault. Ascalon and Tiberias both fell in 1247, but by that time another Crusade would have been launched. The capture of Jerusalem was naturally and inevitably always an emotional lever that could be used by the papacy to rekindle what remained of the Crusading spirit in Europe.

In 1245 Pope Innocent IV preached the Seventh Crusade – but with the curious proviso that the main enemy was not the Moslem but Frederick II, with whom the papacy was once again at daggers drawn. Strangely enough, if it was the Pope who now tried to use Crusading zeal strictly for secular ends, it was left to a layman, Louis IX of France, to restore to the whole concept an indealistic and religious bent. Louis, generally known as St Louis for he was canonised in 1297, was everything that a 'very parfit, gentil knight' was supposed to be – and rarely was. Of him, indeed, the words that Malory puts into the mouth of Sir Ector in his lament over his brother Lancelot might have been written: 'A, Launcelot;' he sayd. 'thou were hede of al Crysten knyghtes!... thou were never matched of erthely knyghtes hand. And thou were the curtest knyght that ever bare sheld: And thou were the truest frende to thy lovar that ever bestrade hors, and thou were the trewest lover, of a synful man, that ever loved woman, and thou were the kyndest man that ever strake with sword. And thou were the godelyest persone that ever came emonge press of knyghtes, and thou was the mekest man and the sternest knyght to thy mortal foo that ever put spere in the reste.'

St Louis took the Cross in the year that Jerusalem fell. It was not for three years that he and his army were to sail. Louis, dedicated, devout, and pious almost to a fault, was also a practical man. He knew that the organisation of fleets and of armies was not something that could be undertaken in the hasty scramble of a few months, or even a year. In those days when communications and road systems were so poor,

Opposite top: *Two Arab horsemen: Baghdad School, c.1210.*
Opposite bottom: *Arabs in a passenger boat: Baghdad School, c.1223.*

Overleaf: *The 1390 French-Genoese expedition to Barbary: fifteenth-century English manuscript.*

allowance always had to be made for something like a fifty per cent delay over what on the face of it might have seemed a reasonable time in which to muster the forces for a Crusade. The sad thing was that, with all his good intentions and with all his sensible forethought, the Crusades led by St Louis were destined to end in failure. He had come too late upon the scene. The whole East was in a ferment, the Ayyubite dynasty in Egypt was soon to fall, and the Latin inhabitants of what was left of the Kingdom were divided, while Frederick's son Conrad was still nominally, through his father, the King of Jerusalem. It was a cat's cradle of dissension, complexity and intrigue out of which no man living could have made a sensible and constructive enterprise.

Louis spent the winter of 1248 in Cyprus, preparing – after due consultation with all the local experts – for an expedition against Egypt in the spring of 1249. It was not in fact until June that the Crusaders got under way. The delay proved fatal to their cause for it had thoroughly alerted the enemy and had given them a chance to summon up reinforcements. Nevertheless the campaign, when finally launched, seemed to have every chance of success. The Crusaders landed, just as John of Brienne had done, with the intention of taking Damietta first of all and then heading south for Cairo. The army consisted of some 20,000 men, of whom nearly 3,000 were knights.

Damietta, unlike the previous occasion, fell without a blow, the garrison and inhabitants fleeing south into Egypt. But, just as on the earlier expedition, the Nile floods were about to begin and Louis, having learned something at least from the lessons of history, was not prepared to be caught as Cardinal Pelagius and John of Brienne had been. The Crusaders settled down to wait. Once again, as Sir Steven Runciman puts it '. . . the Great Mosque became a cathedral and a bishop was installed. Buildings were allotted to the three Military Orders and money benefices to the leading lords of *Outremer*.' The amount of times that churches and mosques changed hands during the turbulent centuries of the Crusades can hardly be calculated. In came the Moslems and expunged all Christian 'idolatrous' paintings and rededicated the churches to unknowable Allah, and then back came the Christians and reinstalled their shrines, their paintings, and their statues. Just as he had done before, Al-Kamil (who was practically on his deathbed from tuberculosis) offered the Christians the return of Jerusalem. Louis, as obdurate in this as Pelagius, turned the offer down. He knew

Opposite: *The Hospitaller Castle of Akkar in the Lebanon, captured by Sultan Baybers in 1271.*

that the hold of the Ayyubite Sultans over Egypt was almost at an end and that the Mameluke Turks were likely to be the next to rule the land, and he felt that during this period of division he could probably succeed where Pelagius had failed.

Only when the waters of the Nile began to recede in October did Louis, now reinforced by his second brother with further troops from France, feel that he could afford to set out on the road south to Mansurah. It was not until the third week of December that, having struggled across the many canals and rivulets which fed into the Nile, the Crusaders were encamped as their predecessors had once been opposite the city, and on the banks of the Bahr-as-Sagir. Once again the impetuosity of the Crusaders and of the Templars was to prove the downfall of the Crusading army. Unwilling to wait for King Louis with the main body of the army to come up behind them, they insisted on an immediate attack on Mansurah. The honour and glory of their Order was all, and, as always, the Templars for their part longed to see some achievement which proved them superior to the Hospitallers, let alone to the new blood from Europe or the other Latin knights from *Outremer*.

A local inhabitant had shown the Crusaders a ford across the Bahr-as-Sagir, and on 7 February the army began to cross. It was a slow and difficult business, and the impetuous who were first across would not wait for the main body of the army to join them. Robert of Artois, the King's brother, despite strict orders from Louis to the contrary, led the attack. At first the element of surprise paid dividends. The Moslem camp was overrun, the commander-in-chief, Fakhr ad-Din, being killed in his bath, and the knights, having stormed through the camp, went at full gallop into Mansurah itself. Had the whole army been with them there can be little doubt that Mansurah would have fallen and the road to Cairo laid open. As it was, it did not take the defenders long to perceive that this was no more than an advance guard of a few hundred men. Under the command of Baybers, so soon to make his name famous throughout the East, they ambushed the mounted men, shot them down from side streets, and finally killed or captured almost every one of them. Robert of Artois was among the dead. The Mamelukes now swept out of the city and engaged the main body of the army, only half of which had managed to cross the river.

A fierce battle took place as the King rallied his forces in the face of the attack. They were severely tried, however, by showers of arrows, for the Mamelukes adopted the old Turkish tactics that had proved so successful in the past, charging up, firing, wheeling round and letting the next line follow. Finally, after the French bowmen had got across, the Moslems withdrew into Mansurah. Louis was now in much the same position as Pelagius had been before him, encamped before the city with, as the days went by, disease spreading throughout the army and provisions running low. In the meantime, the Sultan al-Salih had died, and Louis may have hoped for some palace revolution that would wreck the unity of the enemy. It was not to be. Turanshah, the late Sultan's son, having been proclaimed Sultan in Damascus, returned to Cairo in the February of 1250. Soon afterwards the campaign against the invaders was stepped up, boats being launched into the Nile above their positions and cutting off their supply lines.

By April 1250 it was clear to Louis that the army must extricate itself from what was fast becoming an untenable position. Once again they crossed the river, this time by a precarious bridge, and once again a Crusading army was in retreat back to Damietta. As they struggled up the east bank of the Nile the Moslem horsemen were on them like gadflies. The combination of their incessant stinging attacks as well as

Mongol troops: from Collection of Histories *by Rashid Al-Din, 1306.*

dysentery and typhoid had long reduced the Crusaders to a shadow of the armed might that had swooped down to Mansurah. Then King Louis himself fell ill. The end had come. On 6 April the army surrendered. Joinville, the king's chronicler, maintains that if Louis had not collapsed the army might have got back to Damietta, but probability is against it. They were defeated from the moment that they encamped before the walls of Mansurah.

The end of the Seventh Crusade was tragic in the extreme. The victorious Moslems slaughtered the enemy in their thousands and then, being unwilling to feed what they considered useless mouths, killed three or four hundred prisoners every day. Louis was taken back in chains to Mansurah. His ransom was fixed at a million gold pieces, in return for which he and what remained of his nobles and army might go free. Damietta was to be ceded to the new Sultan. But Turanshah himself was not to survive for very long. A palace revolution, largely inspired by Baybers, led to his assassination and the installation of a Mameluke commander as regent of Egypt. The dynasty established by Saladin was at an end. The Mameluke Turks were the masters of the richest territory in the East.

Mongol troops crossing a frozen river : from Collection of Histories, *by Rashid Al-Din, 1306.*

Mongols and Turks

The revolution in Egypt which led to the end of the Ayyubite dynasty and the installation of a Mameluke Turk as ruler in Cairo was to have far-reaching implications for what remained of the Latin kingdom. Even more ominous for the Christians was the threat from the North posed by the Mongol hordes, whose immense empire had been founded by 'The Conqueror of the World', Genghis Khan, early in the thirteenth century. In his *Histoire des Mongols* Baron d'Ohsson wrote: 'In the track of the Mongols only ruins and human bones are to be seen. Surpassing the most barbarous nations in cruelty, they cut the throats of men, women and children in cold blood. They set fire to the towns and villages, destroy the crops and transform a flourishing countryside into a desert; yet at the same time they are animated neither by hatred nor by vengeance. They scarcely know the names of the people they exterminate.' Of the founder of their empire he also wrote: 'The destruction he wrought spread terror far and wide and deprived the peoples attacked of the courage to defend themselves. Never did a conqueror carry his contempt for humanity to such extremes.'

After the death of Genghis Khan the empire of the Mongols was divided up between his sons, but it was one of his grandsons, Hulagu, who was to have so profound an effect upon the fate and fortunes of the Arabs and the inhabitants of the East. The portion of the Mongol conquests that fell to his lot comprised Persia and Armenia, something which inevitably led him into relations – always hostile – with the Moslems in Syria and Egypt. Now the Mongols at this time were largely Shamanists, or sky-worshippers and, although some of them had been converted to the Moslem faith others, including one of Hulagu's brothers, were either Christian converts or the children of Christian women. It always remained a hope among the Latins in Palestine that they might, by converting one of the Mongol leaders to Christianity, turn the deadly power of these steppe-horsemen to their own advantage, in the same way that the Arabs had managed to utilise the vigour and military prowess of the Turks. Europe, in fact, and especially the Latin inhabitants of *Outremer*, allowed itself to be deluded by the dream of using the Mongols against the Moslems. As it turned out, the Mongols were to lay waste nearly all eastern Europe, pushing their attacks home as far as Vienna, while the Mameluke Sultans of Egypt were to be stirred to renewed activity. The result was that Syria became the battleground where Mongol and Moslem clashed, with inevitably ill effects upon the Latin principalities.

After the collapse of the Crusade, St Louis had elected to remain behind in the Holy Land, trying by every diplomatic means to establish the Kingdom of Jerusalem. Although the Mameluke Sultan of Egypt and the Ayyubite great-grandson of Saladin in Damascus were at daggers drawn, there was little that Louis could do to make use of the situation. He was tempted, naturally enough, to form an alliance with Damascus, but he had also to think of the conditions of the thousands of Franks who were prisoners in Egypt. Finally, in 1254, on the death of his mother Blanche, who had been ruling France as regent in his absence, he was forced by the affairs of his own kingdom to return home. In the meantime Europe was still totally divided in the struggle for power that

'The Conqueror of the World', Genghis Khan, the Mongol Chief.

continued between the papacy and the empire under Frederick. Little at this moment was to be hoped for in terms of large-scale revival of the Crusading impulse, although it must be remembered that, as always and all the time, individuals and individuals with their bands of followers continued to make the voyage to the Levant and to lend their support to the Latins established there. Two years before he left, Louis himself had entertained the prevalent dream of an alliance with the Mongols, and had sent a friar to the court of the Great Khan. As little came of this mission as had come of a previous one sent by the pope, when Khan Quyuq, whose mother was a Christian, had replied to the papal letter admonishing him and requiring him to become a Christian: 'I and my ancestors have been commanded by God to exterminate wicked nations. Am I a Christian? God knows, and if the pope wants to know he had better come and find out.'

In 1260 Hulagu took the first step that definitely threatened the position of the Latins in *Outremer*. Moving out from Persia he invaded Syria and captured Damascus. The Sultan fled south to Egypt to seek refuge with the Mamelukes, then decided that this might prove an even more dangerous cause, and turned north again only to be captured by the Mongols. The Christians during this period could do nothing but sit uneasily on the sidelines as the tides of war washed back and forth. Hulagu's principal general, a Christian called Kitboga, now marched south at his master's bidding to attack Egypt. Had he succeeded the fate of the Latin principalities would have been sealed, with the Mongols standing to the north and south of them. As it was, they were saved for the moment by the very man who in due course was to compass their ruin. Baybers, who by now had become Sultan of Egypt, decisively defeated the Mongol army. Throughout this turbulent perod, if only the Latins had been united, they might have made good use of the warfare that surrounded them. Had they either intervened on the side of the Mongols or, conversely, on that of the Mamelukes, they might in return for their services have obtained the restoration of the Kingdom. But their internal divisions, the 'ancient treachery of the Temple! . . . Long-standing sedition of the Hospitallers!' reduced them to an irritating but ineffective presence which was in due course to provoke the hostility of Mongols and Moslems alike.

After crushing the Mongols Baybers swept on north and seized Damascus. The two great capitals of the East, Cairo and Damascus, were once more reunited as they had been in the days of Saladin. A crescent of power now stretched all round the coastal area in which the last of the Latins squabbled over their petty kingdoms. Meanwhile the

Genoese and Venetians, upon whom *Outremer* was dependent for its shipping and transport, were engaged in a bitter commercial war. This was to end with the Genoese allying themselves with the Greek Palaeologi dynasty and overthrowing the Latin kingdom of Constantinople.

Baybers was not the man to miss the opportunities presented to him by the dissensions in the ranks of these European interlopers in the East. A brilliant soldier, a capable administrator, and as fanatical a Moslem as Saladin had been, he had all his predecessor's qualities save those of chivalry, courtesy, or kindness. Where Saladin had represented the flower of Moslem culture, Baybers was at heart a Turk from the steppes of Asia. In 1265, having reinforced the Moslem castles in Syria, giving as his reason that he expected a further Mongol invasion, he suddenly turned his army into Palestine. Caesarea and Arsuf fell before him, all the defenders being put to the sword and the walls razed to the ground. In the following year, the strategically important fortress of Safad surrendered to him, on the condition that the garrison was to go free, unarmed and taking no possessions with them. Baybers agreed and then, when they had all marched out, killed them to a man. Here was a Sultan who had no intention of allowing any sentiment or code of honour to stand in the way of his ultimate objective – the expulsion of all Christians from the East.

In 1268 Baybers once more moved up from Egypt and the great city of Jaffa felt the wind of his sword. The walls of this famous and ancient trading port were razed to the ground, such inhabitants as were not killed or enslaved were all expelled, and Baybers made certain of the security of the city by planting a Turkish colony on the site. Moving northwards past Tripoli (which he might have been wiser to besiege) the Sultan laid waste all the surrounding territory – some of the richest and most fertile land in *Outremer* – and by May had advanced as far as Antioch. This former Roman capital of the East had long been among the most prosperous of Latin possessions, and a great centre of trade between the Orient and Europe. It fell to Baybers after a siege of only four days. The city where Antony and Cleopatra had once wintered, Antioch rich in commerce and adorned with innumerable art treasures from the ancient world, was handed over to the Turkish Mamelukes to loot and destroy. Every male inhabitant was butchered, and the women and children were sold into slavery. Then, as with Jaffa, the city was razed to the ground. In empty and non-productive violence there was little to choose between the Mongol and the Turk.

At this moment it would seem that Baybers could easily have completed his mission and captured all the remaining Latin castles and

Mongol court procession, where nobles and court officials surround their chieftain : early fourteenth-century manuscript.

fortified places and driven the Christians out of the East once and for all. It is possible that he was concerned about rumours that St Louis was raising another Crusade, and was afraid of a large force landing south of him and making for Egypt. It is more likely, however, that the reason why he desisted was that he had other preoccupations, notably the Armenian kingdom of Cilicia, which he proceeded to lay waste in his usual fashion, killing some 60,000 Christians and enslaving thousands more. Prior to this he had concluded a ten-year truce with Acre, which gave the city a breathing space before its ultimate and inevitable end. Meanwhile, hearing of the terrifying progress of Baybers in the East, St Louis had once again taken the Cross. Many of the French nobles, including the King's own historian Joinville, refused to follow him, one of his only imitators being Prince Edward of England, later to be King Edward I. In the summer of 1270, under the mistaken apprehension that the Bey of Tunis might be converted, St Louis directed his Crusade, the Eighth Crusade, against Tunis, but hardly had he landed than he sickened and died. His last words are said to have been 'Jerusalem, Jerusalem!' His brother Charles, who arrived shortly afterwards, managed to negotiate successfully, somewhat in the spirit of Frederick

217

II, and secured the payment of a large indemnity from the Bey which served to bolster up the finances both of France and of Sicily, of which Charles was now king. The saintly Crusader Louis – the last in the 'grand manner' of the early Crusades – had, despite all his intelligence and his virtues, achieved little. With his death the last sunset glow of the Crusades flickers against the gathering dark.

Prince Edward, who had arrived after the conclusion of the treaty, which in his Crusading zeal he regarded as a betrayal of all true values, moved on in 1271 to Acre. Although he had only a small force with him, the threat of a major action was sufficient to cause Baybers to conclude a ten-year truce with the city. Edward spent over a year at Acre, at the conclusion of which he was able to negotiate a further ten-year treaty between Sultan Baybers and Hugh III, who was King of Cyprus and titular King of Jerusalem. In 1271, however, the great Hospitaller castle Krak des Chevaliers had fallen to the victorious Sultan, thus sounding the death knell of the Hospitallers in the Holy Land and the Levant. Treaties notwithstanding, the Mameluke Sultan was left in effective control of the whole area, the Latins in the East only remaining on his sufferance. Edward left for England in 1272. The last of the western Crusaders of any note, he had only escaped from the East by good fortune with his life when an assassin, allegedly sent by Baybers, stabbed him with a poisoned dagger while he lay asleep. The story went that his wife Eleanor saved him from death by sucking the poison from his wound. But the poison – to *Outremer* at any rate – that was never to be eliminated, was Baybers himself.

Saracen warrior armed with scimitar, short bow, and shield.

The Fall of Acre

Baybers died in June 1277 aged fifty-five. A great soldier, a man who would never ask his troops to do what he could not do himself, always foremost in the trenches, siting and laying the siege engines or directng the battering rams, foremost in every cavalry charge, he was a man who had lived always in an atmosphere where 'battle, murder and sudden death' seemed like his signature. His death left Egypt temporarily without a ruler, and the elevation of his son, Baraka, to the sultanate was not to last long for, as is often the case, the son was only a dim shadow of his father. The last years of Baybers, surely one of the greatest sultans despite all his defects and cruelties, were crowned with success. In the very year of his death he defeated a combination of Seljuk Turks and Mongols and shortly afterwards made a triumphal entry into Caesarea which, along with so many other famous cities of the East, now joined the empire that he had created.

Qalaun, who had been regent of Egypt during the minority of Baybers' second son, was finally by the expressed will of the Mamelukes elevated to the sultanate. Like Baybers, he was a Turk who had been brought to Egypt as a slave and had risen solely by his own merits to this supreme position in the Moslem world. Like Baybers also he proceeded to hold back the Mongols and, by concluding a ten-year treaty with the Franks in 1281, managed to keep them pacified until such time as he had dealt with his major foes, the horsemen from the steppes of Asia. Well aware that the Latins in *Outremer* were only waiting for an opportunity to turn the power of the Mongols against Egypt and the Moslem world. Qalaun bided his time until there was a lull in his warfare against the Mongols and Tatars. He then turned his attention to his Christian enemies. In 1285, the great Hospitaller fortress of Margat (Marqab) fell after a siege that had lasted over a month, and which could have lasted for far longer but for the fact that, due to the circumstances of the time, the castle was undermanned. The knights had also been relying upon the fact that the ten-year truce was still in existence, but Qalaun was no more to be relied upon than Baybers himself had been. He did what suited him. The defenders, unmolested, were permitted to leave for Tripoli, that great commercial port which was one of the last substantial holdings of the Latins in the East.

During these years, when the ultimate extinction of *Outremer* must have been clear to any dispassionate onlooker, there had still been attempts at rekindling the Crusading fire in Europe. In 1274 Pope Gregory X had preached the Crusade and all the princes of western Europe had taken the Cross. The Pope had also managed to reconcile the Eastern and Western Churches and had secured the aid of the Palaeologi who were now the rulers of Constantinople. All was to no avail, for on the death of Gregory two years later the Crusade died with him. In 1278 Charles of Anjou, who had established himself in Acre, attempted to revive the disastrous spirit which had animated the Fourth Crusade and reclaim Constantinople for the Latins. His aims were thwarted primarily by the uprising in Sicily known as the Sicilian Vespers. This was to lead in due course to the establishment of an Aragonese dynasty in that great central island of the Mediterranean. In 1286, in a hollow ceremony in Acre, Henry II of Cyprus was crowned King, and a fortnight of games, festivals and tournaments was held as if the Kingdom of Jerusalem still existed, as if *Outremer* was as it had been all those many decades ago, and as if the Kings of Europe and the noblest of the Normans till clamoured to restore the holy places. All had changed. Hardly visible as yet, but casting a long shadow before it, modern Europe was on the horizon.

In the following year, on the death of Bohemund VII, Count of Tripoli, the citizens opted for a republic, and asked the Genoese, themselves repulicans, to send a fleet and give weight to their aspirations. Genoa was only too willing to oblige, for the great port of Tripoli would give her a decided advantage in the Levant over her two hated rivals, the Pisans and the Venetians. Qalaun, for his part, was more than unwilling to see any of the great Italian maritime powers established at Tripoli. In 1289, once again happily forgetting that 'scrap of paper', the ten-year truce, he arrived with an army consisting of thousands of cavalry and foot-soldiers, as well as a great siege train and hundreds of expert Egyptian sappers and miners. Within a month the city fell to a general assault,

Opposite: *The Fall of Acre : from* Vie et Miracles de Saint Louis, *early fifteenth-century manuscript.*

and the whole surrounding country was in Moslem hands. The city and port, one of the chief manufacturing centres in the East as well as all-important in the trade between Europe and the Orient, was razed to the ground and its citizens indiscriminately slaughtered. Qalaun intended to leave nothing behind, not even dockyard or harbour installations, which could possibly be used by any further Crusaders coming from the West.

Nothing of any consequence was now left but Acre. This ancient harbour-town, situated at so strategic a point on the main military high-way along the coast, had been the subject of innumerable sieges over the centuries, sieges going as far back as one successfully carried out by Pharaoh Thutmose II in 1500 BC. It was now destined to come under attack by the Mameluke rulers of Egypt. Qalaun himself died in 1290 at the age of seventy while mustering an army for the siege of Acre. He was succeeded by his son Khalil, who was equally determined to complete his father's work – the expulsion of the last of the Franks from the East. The city was defended by a double line of walls within which there was a garrison force of 800 knights and 14,000 foot-soldiers. Against this the Sultan brought up an army at least five times the size – some chroniclers maintain ten times – and the heaviest siege train on record, consisting of over ninety mangonels and *trebuchets* as well as all the equipment for manufacturing towers and other devices. *Trebuchets* were giant cata-pults throwing a mass of rock from the end of a long revolving arm, the motive power being provided by a counter-weight at the short end of the arm. The *mangonel*, used constantly in sieges throughout the Middle Ages, looked rather like a giant spoon and was operated by a windlass. It was used not only for hurling rocks and stones but incendiary missiles – Greek fire – contained in pottery jars which burst on impact. On 11 April, 1291, the siege of Acre began.

The defences of the city were manned according to national groupings or by detachments of the Military Orders. Thus, the Templars held the northern sector of the city walls within which was the great fortified palace of their Order. The Hospitallers were to their right, while to the right of the Hospitallers again were the knights and men from Syria and Cyprus. On the southern line of the defences was stationed a French and an English contingent, while Pisans, Genoese, and Venetians, as befitted their trade as sailors, held the area just above the port itself. On the fourth night of the siege the Grand Master of the Temple, supported by the English, led out a mounted detachment and made a successful raid from the Porte St Lazaire, the northern gate of the city, inflicting considerable damage upon the Moslems. They failed however in their main objective, the capture and destruction of the siege weapons which were daily eroding the defences. A few nights later, equally eager to prove their aggressive spirit, the Hospitallers made a sortie aimed at the centre of the Moslem camp. This time, however, having learned from their previous experience, the enemy were armed, ready and waiting. The Hospitallers were forced to withdraw without having accomplished anything.

Day after day, while the incendiaries whirled overhead to burst on the rooftops of Acre, and while the walls spurted dust and crumbled under the lash of limestone rocks, the sappers were busy. Before the use of gunpowder, it was usually by sapping and mining that a breach was made

A hefty catapult hurls rocks at a Moslem garrison under siege: thirteenth-century French manuscript.

in the walls of a city or fortress of sufficient size to permit a major assault. The technique was simple but effective, the shafts and galleries of the miners being propped up by wooden beams. Finally, when calculations showed that the head of the tunnel was underneath the desired section of wall, a great fire was lit while the workmen scuttled back to safety. When the pit-props and struts caught fire down came the tunnel, aided in its fall by the weight of the masonry above it. At Acre the first parts to begin to crack and crumble were the towers of the English, of Blois, and of St Nicholas. Then, on 15 May, the new tower named after Henry II came down in part-ruin, to be overrun shortly afterwards by a concerted

Trebuchet, a giant catapult used throughout the Middle Ages.

Mameluke attack. The defenders, abandoning the outer line of the walls, were now forced back within the inner circuit of defences.

On 18 May the Sultan gave the order for the general assault. The attack was launched before dawn along the whole length of the walls, the main weight being directed at what was known as the Accursed Tower. This was at the angle of the salient of the eastern wall and was held by knights from Syria and Cyprus. Preceding the attack, the entire armament of the besiegers had opened up in a massive concentration of fire, while the air was darkened by a blizzard of arrows. Then, to the rumbling thunder of the Turkish drums, the Mamelukes came to the

From a thirteenth-century English manuscript.

charge. Advancing in deep columns the attackers swept all resistance
before them. By sunrise Moslem banners were fluttering in many places
along the walls while advance columns were even beginning to overrun
the inner line of the city's defences. William of Beaujeu, Grand Master
of the Templars, was killed in the onslaught that fell upon the Accursed
Tower, and the Grand Master of the Hospitallers, John of Villiers, was
so seriously wounded that, despite his protestations, his men insisted on
taking him down to the harbour and putting him aboard one of the
waiting ships. In the assault that fell upon the long area of the wall
running north from the Gate of St Anthony, Templars and Hospitallers
fought side by side, all divisions and dissensions of the past forgotton.
But had those same divisions and dissensions never existed it is just
possible that the fate of the Kingdom might have been a different one.
At any rate, 'in their death they were not divided . . .' Acre was lost.
Nearly all the Hospitallers were killed and the Templars, who had
retreated into their palace at the northern tip of the promontory,
managed to hold out for a further week before they too were overwhelmed in the smoking ruin.

By the night of 18 May the whole of the city with the exception of the
Templars' palace was in the hands of the Sultan Khalil. The original
population was said to have been in the region of 40,000, but this had
undoubtedly been swollen by sailors, soldiers, and refugees, prior to
the siege. Out of all these few were to survive, the shipping being insufficient to take off more than a relatively small percentage. The
massacre was similar to those enacted in cities previously captured by
the Mamelukes. Ten thousand prisoners were killed on the Sultan's
orders alone. Acre – its fortifications, walls, towers, houses, warehouses,
and port installations – was set afire and demolished. In the days following the fall of the city, Beirut, Tyre, Haifa, and Tortosa were evacuated.
There were no more Latin settlements in the East, no proud castles like
Krak des Chevaliers, no fortified cities so strangely combining a Norman-
Moslem culture.

The Mamelukes brought nothing to replace what they had destroyed.
The Christians were expelled, but the Moslem civilization of which
Saladin was the epitome was not to flower on the ruins of the land.
Thousands of Christians glutted the slave markets of the East, the price
of a nubile girl dropping as low as a simple drachma. The Crusades were
over. The dream of *Outremer* was over. Far away in Cyprus the refugees
in their pitiable distress served as a living reminder to Greeks and
Franks alike that the Latin Kingdom of the East was at an end – for ever.

The great Hospitaller fortress of Margat (Marqab) in Syria: set on a steep triangular hill, the castle was admirable for defence.

After the Sunset

The loss of Acre, the collapse of *Outremer*, the triumph of the Moslems, none of these things could arouse a Europe that was fully occupied with national wars and rivalries. The whole moral and intellectual climate of the continent had changed so completely since 1100 that the Crusades died from inanition. It is true that, as late as 1365, King Peter of Cyprus, having failed to arouse any interest among the sovereigns of Europe, attempted his own Crusade, sacking Alexandria and ravaging Syria. His assassination four years later removed for ever from the scene the last of the real Crusaders. Attempts were made by the Venetians from the mid-fourteenth century onwards to curb the power of the Ottoman Turks, but in the long run they too were destined to fail. The fact remains that the idea of the Crusades, the dream of once more recapturing Jerusalem and restoring a Christian kingdom in the Holy Land, continued to haunt men's minds for centuries to come. That great founder of Portuguese seapower, the man who more than any other set in train the conquest of the Atlantic, Prince Henry the Navigator, thought constantly of turning the riches that should accrue to his country into a new Crusade to liberate Jerusalem. He died before the success of the Portuguese navigators in finding the sea-route to India had made his dream an economic possibility, and his successors were practical men without his medieval cast of thought.

It was, indeed, the very success of European oceanic navigation that finally and forever extinguished the continent's interest in Egypt and the Levant. The Ottoman Empire, which lay like a scimitar across the whole of the eastern Mediterranean, was circumvented. Trade between Europe and the Far East now flowed through the veins of caravels and

Opposite: *The Hospitallers prepare to defend Rhodes against the Turks in 1480: from a late fifteenth-century manuscript.*

square-rigged merchantmen. Yet it is worth bearing in mind that even as late as 1492 that great Genoese seaman, Christopher Columbus, prayed as he set foot in the New World that its riches might be used to liberate Jerusalem.

Of the three great Military Orders whose history is part and parcel of the Crusades, only the Hospitallers were to continue to make their mark upon the East, and to continue right into the eighteenth century their dedicated warfare upon the Moslem. The reason for this is not so hard to find: the Hospitallers, demoralised though they were in the years immediately following the loss of *Outremer*, still had their vocation. The vows that enjoined them to be servants of the poor and the sick could be – and were – carried out in Cyprus, where one of their first actions was to build a new hospital. Afterwards, when they had made their home in Rhodes (where they stayed for over two centuries until finally expelled by the Turks), they resumed their military activities against the Moslems. But this time it was as fighting seamen that they haunted the routes of the East, or made commando-type raids upon the coastlines of Asia Minor and the Levant. Their ardour unquenched by their expulsion from Rhodes, they went to Malta in 1530 where they perfected their organisation, built some of the greatest fortress-architecture the world has ever seen, and proceeded in 1565 to defeat the whole might of the Ottoman Empire when it was unleashed against Malta in that action which has rightly become known as 'The Great Siege'. For over two centuries, until their submission to Napoleon in 1798, the members of the Order not only maintained the finest hospital in Europe but fought constantly against the Moslems in almost every action that took place in the Mediterranean. They were prominent in the Battle of Lepanto, resisted to the last alongside the Venetians in the famous siege of Candia in Crete, and constantly took part in land and sea operations against the Moslems in North Africa. They alone still survive to this day, carrying out world-wide hospitaller activities, and having their headquarters in Rome.

The Templars, being a purely military organisation, were less capable of adapting, and were destined for extinction. Their great wealth inevitably provoked the cupidity of others while their great power also provoked the hostility of kings. In 1307, when Jacques de Molay, the Grand Master, as well as nearly all the other Templars were in France, King Philip of France seized the opportunity and struck. All the Templars were arrested on charges of blasphemy and heresy. Endless debate has arisen around the subject, as to whether the charges were trumped up or had some origin in fact. It is not impossible that some of the accusa-

Effigy of a Templar knight, in the Temple Church, London.

tions were true but, true or not, the extinction of the Order and the
seizure of its property and lands suited Philip very well. A large part of
the wealth and possessions of the Order, however, was beyond Philip's
grasp and all of this was transferred to the Order of St John. In the end,
it was the Hospitallers who were mainly to benefit by the extinction of
their former great rival.

A very different fate was reserved for the Teutonic Order which,

231

after the expulsion from *Outremer*, went on to take its Crusading zeal
not against the Moslem but against the pagan Prussians. The German
knights were, in fact, the spearhead of the colonisation of Prussia and,
since their avowed aim was to Christianise the heathen, their warfare
was regarded by the Popes as a form of Crusade. Ultimately they became
a politico-military organisation which administered vast estates in the
conquered territory. In some respects they represent the first impulse of
that German *Drang nach Osten* which was to end in Hitler's invasion of
Russia in the Second World War. The Order itself, to all intents and
purposes, came to an end in 1410 when it was overwhelmed at Tannen-
berg in East Prussia by King Ladislaus of Poland.

The Crusades can be looked at in two basic ways. It is easy enough to
see in them a vivid play which depicts the spectacle of man's folly,
greed, and capacity for self-destruction. All that is true. There is another
side, however, and one which it is important not to overlook. If, as has
been said, 'they touched the summits of daring and devotion', it must
be admitted that they also sank into the depths of shame. But, over and

The Burning of the Templars: fourteenth-century manuscript.

232

above all that, they represented part of the phenomenon that is man –
the capacity to dare all for the sake of an ideal. Though it would be true
to say that comparatively few of the Europeans who took part in the
Crusades had any real conception of what was implied by the life of the
Founder of their religion, yet it would be false to deny that very many of
them were truly dedicated to the dream of creating the kingdom of God
upon earth. The fact that the means adopted for this end were, more
often than not, violent, bloody, and treacherous, does not detract from
the hoped-for end which drove millions of men to leave their homes and
endure incredible suffering on their pilgrimage towards the Holy Land.
The resistance of the Moslems to what they regarded as a heretical
doctrine must equally be seen as being motivated by the noblest of
impulses. In the end, through its acquisition of new flowers and fruits,
new crafts and manufactures, new aspects of philosophy and mathe-
matics, to name but a few things, it was the West that gained from this
turbulent cross-pollination with the East. The Crusades remain as vivid
as forked-lightning against a dark sky. They presage the Renaissance.
They are not ignoble.

*The Crusader returns and takes off his heavy armour : from one of three poems on
pilgrimages by Guillaume de Deguileville, a monk of Chaalis in Valois, c.1340.*

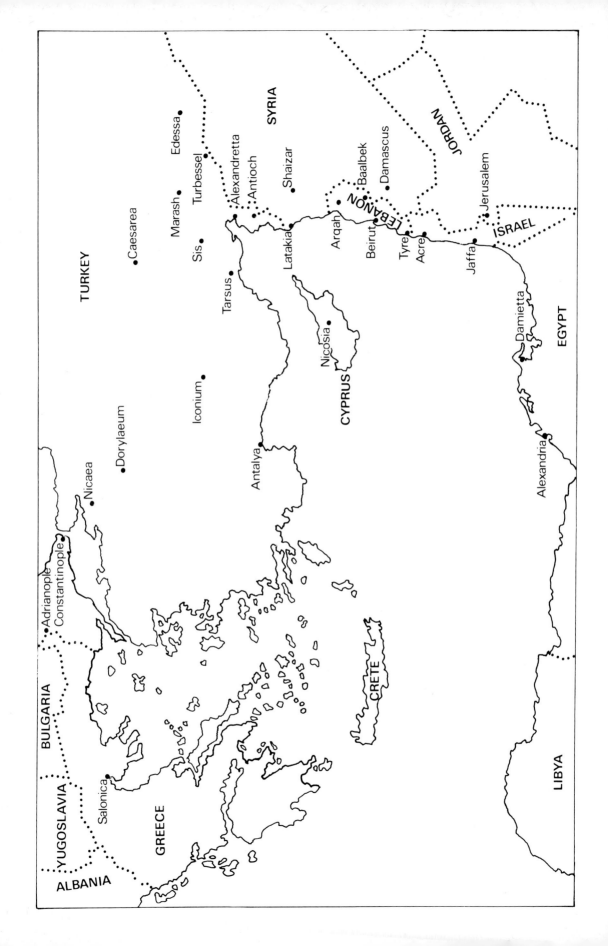

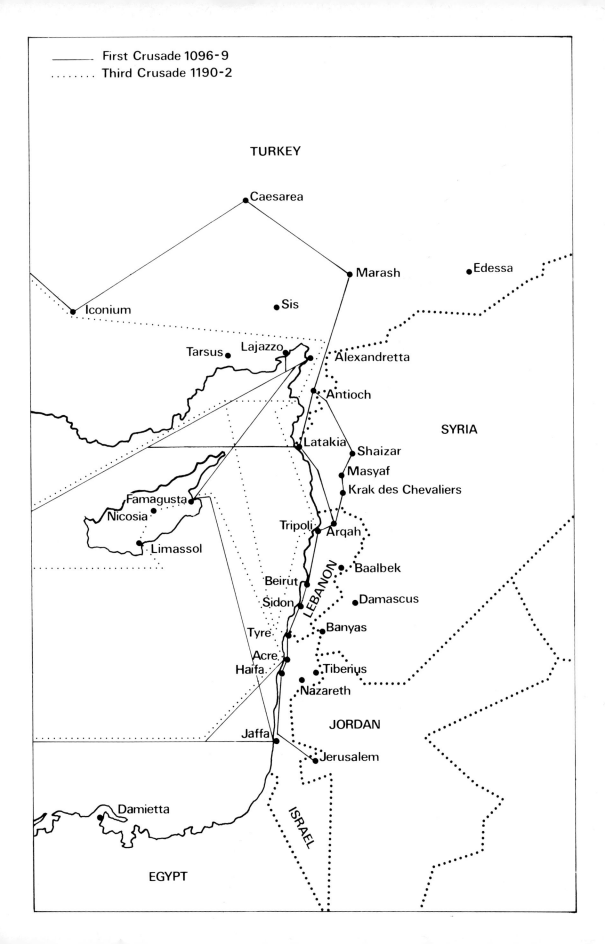

First Crusade 1096-9

.... Third Crusade 1190-2

TURKEY

Caesarea

Marash

Edessa

Iconium

Sis

Tarsus

Lajazzo

Alexandretta

Antioch

SYRIA

Latakia

Shaizar

Masyaf

Krak des Chevaliers

Famagusta

Nicosia

Tripoli

Arqah

Limassol

Baalbek

Beirut

LEBANON

Sidon

Damascus

Tyre

Banyas

Acre

Haifa

Tiberius

Nazareth

JORDAN

Jaffa

Jerusalem

Damietta

ISRAEL

EGYPT

Index

The publishers wish to express their thanks to the following museums, libararies and other institutions from whose collections works have been reproduced: Art Gallery and Museum, Glasgow, 94 centre; Biblioteca Nacional, Madrid, 159; Biblioteca Trivulziana, Milan, 199; Bibliotheque Nationale, Paris, jacket, 17, 18, 20, 25, 33, 39, 48, 59, 61, 66, 74 top, 76, 81, 91, 92, 106, 143, 162, 184, 200, 205, 221, 223, 228; Bodleian Library, Oxford, 40 (mss Douce 217f77), 64 (mss Tanner 190f22), 70 (mss Tanner 190f189), 140 (mss Tanner 190f17), 167 (mss Laud 587); The Trustees of the British Museum, London, 2, 36, 45, 51, 57, 63, 74 bottom, 82, 88, 120, 149, 152, 169, 194, 206, 232, 233; Burgerbibliothek, Bern, 157; The Governing Body of Christ Church, Oxford, 224; Cluny Museum, Paris, 26; The Master and Fellows of Corpus Christi College, Cambridge, 99, 124, 129, 144, 151, 186, 188, 191, 196, 202; Edinburgh University Library, 89, 101, 211, 212; Her Majesty's Stationery Office, London, 94 right, 97 right; Kunsthistorisches Museum, Vienna, 94 left; The Metropolitan Museum of Art, New York, 170; Musee Municipale, Limoges, 13; Pierpont Morgan Library, New York, (ms. 638) 102, 113, 117, 192, 198; Royal Library, The Hague, 83; Topkapi Saray Museum, Istanbul, 205; The Master and Fellows of Trinity College, Cambridge, 96; Universitatsbibliothek, Jena, 30; Vatican Library, 181; The Trustees of Wallace Collection, London, 97 left.

All photographs reproduced, with the exception of those listed below, are from the Park and Roche Establishment archives (photographers M. Carrieri and Alexandr Paul).

Alinari, Florence, 109; Archives Photographiques, Paris, endpaper, 52, 183; Boudot-Lamotte, Paris, 114; Mr F. H. Crossley, 125; Giraudon, Paris, 59, 126, 178; A. F. Kersting, London, 43, 46, 118, 131, 132, 174, 208, 227, 231; Mansell Collection, London, 7, 8, 23, 85, 123, 136, 165, 177, 217, 218; Michael Holford Library, London, 73; Radio Times Hulton Picture Library, London, 10, 79, 197, 214; Scala, Florence, 35, 69, 181; Snark International, Paris, 172.

BIBLIOGRAPHY

The Knight and Chivalry, Richard Barber, 1970.
The Crusades, Sir Ernest Barker, 1929.
The Shield and the Sword, Ernle Bradford, 1972.
Le Crac des Chevaliers, P Deschamps, 1934.
Crusader Castles, R Fedden, 1950.
The Course of Empire, Sir John Glubb, 1965.
The Empire of the Arabs, Sir John Glubb, 1963.
History of Cyprus, G Hill, 1948.
The Knights Hospitaller in the Holy Land, E J King, 1931.
Anthology of Arabic Literature, (Ed) James Kritzeck, 1964.
Mahommedan Dynasties, S Lane-Poole, 1894.
Saladin, S Lane-Poole, 1903.
Les Français d'Outremer au Moyen Age, J Lognon, 1929.
Richard the Lion Heart, K Norgate, 1924.
A History of the Crusades (3 vols), Sir Steven Runciman, 1951.
History of the Byzantine Empire, A A Vasiliev, 1952.

Histoire de l'Empire Ottoman, J Von Hammer, 1841.
The Wars of Religion, Cambridge Modern History, Vol III, 1907.

Chronicles

Historia Hierosolymitana, William of Tyre, (Ed) M N Colvin, 1893.
La Conquête de Constantinople, Villehardouin, (Ed) Faral, 1938.
Gesta Francorum, (Ed) Hagenmeyer, 1890.
Historia Pontificalis quae Supersunt, (Ed) S Lane-Poole, 1927.
La Conquête de Constantinople, Robert de Clari, (Ed) Lauer, 1924.
Histoire de Saint Louis, Joinville, (Ed) Wailly, 1874.
De Profectione Ludovici VII in Orientem, (Ed) Waquet, 1949.